Praise for *The Bo*

"*[The Book That Changed M*y ... approach in this collection of 7 ... welcoming and inspiring book ... teens
curious about books and writers, or in need of an unthreatening invitation to experience the pleasures of books." —*Booklist*

"What I love about *The Book That Changed My Life* is the way it captures a passion that has been muted by earthly concerns about money and competition and sell-through; like a lot of us, these authors clearly love books and its biz." —Sara Nelson, *Publishers Weekly*

"[A] wonderful cross section of contributors and a wildly diverse group of books. From the Bible (Senator Joseph Lieberman) to *To Kill a Mockingbird* (author Wally Lamb), the contents of this book will encourage quick perusal, a checking of titles, or the generation of a must-read list." —STARRED *Library Journal*

"Bet you can't read just one." —*The Hartford Courant*

"The 71 authors offer . . . happy hoorays and heartfelt blessings. . . ."
—*The Boston Globe*

"After years of hosting authors and writers of every caliber, level of fame, and expertise, Roxanne Coady has finally joined their ranks."
—*New Haven Register*

"Editor Joy Johannessen and bookseller Roxanne Coady have gathered together a star-studded roster of authors . . . [whose] passion for their books is downright contagious, making you want to rush to the shelves to pay homage to your own personal bests."
—*Cookie Magazine*

"[A] stunning collection of original essays." —*Pages*

"A Connecticut bookseller and a New York publishing vet corral an impressive assemblage of noted writers to contribute brief essays on the one book they will forever remember. Many of the pairings of writer and book are delightfully unexpected (Nelson DeMille on Ayn Rand's *Atlas Shrugged*!). Of course, many classics appear among the favorites, but this anthology also contains many remarkable books that merit rediscovery, such as Sebastian Junger on Dee Brown's *Bury My Heart at Wounded Knee*." —*Seattle Post-Intelligencer*

Tricia Bohan Photography

Roxanne J. Coady is the founder of R.J. Julia Booksellers in Madison, Connecticut. R.J. Julia hosts over two hundred author events each year, and won the *Publishers Weekly* Bookseller of the Year Award in 1995. In 1996, Coady and a small group of women founded the Read to Grow Foundation, which provides books and literacy information to tens of thousands of newborns and their families each year. Roxanne is a regular guest on Public Radio and has appeared on *Good Morning America* and *The Today Show*. She lives in Connecticut with her husband and son.

Joy Johannessen has been an editor/executive editor at Grove Press, Oxford University Press, HarperCollins, and Delphinium Books. Among the writers she has worked with are Dorothy Allison, Harold Bloom, Michael Cunningham, Nien Cheng, Ursula Le Guin, and Arthur Miller. She lives in upstate New York.

THE BOOK THAT CHANGED MY LIFE

71 Remarkable Writers Celebrate the Books That Matter Most to Them

EDITED BY
ROXANNE J. COADY
AND JOY JOHANNESSEN

GOTHAM BOOKS

GOTHAM BOOKS
Published by Penguin Group (USA) Inc.
375 Hudson Street, New York, New York 10014, U.S.A.

Penguin Group (Canada), 90 Eglinton Avenue East, Suite 700, Toronto, Ontario, Canada M4P 2Y3 (a division of Pearson Penguin Canada Inc.); Penguin Books Ltd, 80 Strand, London WC2R 0RL, England; Penguin Ireland, 25 St Stephen's Green, Dublin 2, Ireland (a division of Penguin Books Ltd); Penguin Group (Australia), 250 Camberwell Road, Camberwell, Victoria 3124, Australia (a division of Pearson Australia Group Pty Ltd); Penguin Books India Pvt Ltd, 11 Community Centre, Panchsheel Park, New Delhi–110 017, India; Penguin Group (NZ), 67 Apollo Drive, Rosedale, North Shore 0745, Auckland, New Zealand (a division of Pearson New Zealand Ltd); Penguin Books (South Africa) (Pty) Ltd, 24 Sturdee Avenue, Rosebank, Johannesburg 2196, South Africa

Penguin Books Ltd, Registered Offices: 80 Strand, London WC2R 0RL, England

Published by Gotham Books, a division of Penguin Group (USA) Inc.

Previously published as a Gotham Books hardcover edition, October 2006

First trade paperback printing, October 2007

1 3 5 7 9 10 8 6 4 2

Gotham Books and the skyscraper logo are trademarks of Penguin Group (USA) Inc.

THE LIBRARY OF CONGRESS HAS CATALOGUED THE HARDCOVER EDITION OF THE BOOK AS FOLLOWS:
The book that changed my life : 71 remarkable writers celebrate the books that matter most to them / edited by Roxanne J. Coady and Joy Johannessen.
p. cm.
ISBN 1-592-40210-0 (hardcover) ISBN 978-1-592-40317-2 (paperback)
1. Authors, American—20th century—Books and reading. 2. Authorship. I. Coady, Roxanne J. II. Johannessen, Joy.
Z1039.A87B65 2006
028'.8—dc22 2006023179

Printed in the United States of America
Set in Bembo with Bank Gothic • Designed by Sabrina Bowers

In memory of my father and in honor of my mother
—R. J. C.

For the friends who saved me
—J. J.

Contents

INTRODUCTION

ROXANNE J. COADY

It's funny that reading and valuing words is now what anchors my life. When my mother first read to me, neither she nor I, her two-year-old listener, understood the words. She was a recent immigrant from Hungary and hadn't learned English yet, but she "read" to me almost every day. She just sounded out the words phonetically, and mostly that worked, except we thought *know* was *ka-now* and *high* was *hig-ha.* Actually, it isn't surprising that I grew up to value words—my mother snuggling up with me, reading in her beautiful voice, both of us enjoying the illustrations, trying to figure out the story, making up the story. It really was all about words, and my earliest pleasure was about those books, even just holding them—or catching them.

My brother Gary was born in 1955 at Jewish Memorial Hospital on 197th Street in New York City. In those days, children were not allowed on the maternity floor, so my dad brought me and my sister Barbara around to the side of the hospital to "visit" our mother, and there she was, four floors up, smiling down at us. As was her nature, she had gifts for us. From the window that day she dropped two Golden Books, one for me and one for Barbara. I think it was at that moment, with books falling from the sky, that the notion solidified in my six-year-old mind that books were from heaven.

As I grew older, I read incessantly, to the point of exasperating even my mother when I was lost in a book and therefore ignoring any tasks she had in mind for me. Through high school and college and beyond, I found myself always excited to talk with friends about the books I was reading, always eager to hear about what they were reading, and inevitably lending my books out all the time. Reading was my passion. Although I ended up majoring in finance and accounting and tax law, I was a bookseller at heart, and after a twenty-year detour as a tax accountant, I came back to books. I left New York and my job as national tax director for BDO Seidman, moved to Madison, Connecticut, and opened R.J. Julia Booksellers. My dream was that the store would be a place where words mattered, where people would gather, where writer could meet reader, and where our staff would work hard to put the right book in the right hand.

Dreams can come true. R.J. Julia has now been welcoming readers and writers for sixteen years. Every day in the store we see how books change lives, in big ways and small, from the simple desire to spend a few quiet hours in a comfy chair, swept away by a story, to the profound realization that the reader is not alone in the world, that there is someone else like him or her, someone who has faced the same fears, the same confusions, the same grief, the same joys. Reading is a way to live more lives, to experience more worlds, to meet people we care about and want to know more about, to understand others and develop a compassion for what they confront and endure. It is a way to learn how to knit or build a house or solve an equation, a way to be moved to laughter and wonder and to learn how to live.

Watching R.J.'s customers, I've seen beyond doubt what books can do for them. I've begun to feel that in all our fascination with technology we've forgotten that a simple book can make a difference. We are still the same people we've always been, and the fact that we live in a high-tech world has not changed our emotions and needs. Time after time, when authors come to the store to read, I hear members of the audience tell them how their books evoke those emotions and speak to those needs. One summer night in 1994, with the temperature in the nineties and the store's air conditioning broken, Pete Hamill read to a packed room from *A Drinking Life* and stayed on for hours as one person after another came up to shake his hand or touch his arm and say that his book made them feel understood at last, as if he had told *their* story. When we hosted Alice Sebold for *The Lovely Bones*, a cop stood up to thank her for her first book, *Lucky*, her memoir of being raped. His wife had been raped, he said, and Alice had given her a voice at a time when she couldn't find her own. These are just two stories among hundreds. Everything I have observed in the store over the years has confirmed the love of books my mother awakened in me as she read to me in her halting phonetic English.

But not every child is so fortunate. In 1996 a local health clinic asked us to help replenish the "gently used" books they gave out to children who came to the clinic. With the support of our readers, our staff, and our community, we filled two school buses with twelve thousand books. In expressing the clinic's appreciation, pediatrician Laurel Shader told us what it was like to see an eight-year-old boy's expression upon receiving the first book he ever owned. For a minute I thought I hadn't understood her. Connecticut has the highest per capita income in the country, and I was staggered by the realization that there were children—turns out there are thousands of children—who have never owned a book. This had to change. In 1997 a small group of us got together and formed a nonprofit organization called Read to Grow, which started with the simple idea that every baby born in our local hospital, Yale-New Haven, would receive a new book.

Read to Grow has since evolved into a vibrant organization that promotes literacy and the joy of reading through direct contact with families. Read to Grow now has two major components: Books for Babies, which has distributed seventeen thousand new books to newborns in seven urban hospitals in the last year, along with a packet for parents on why and how to read to their infants; and Books for Kids, which provides ongoing support for family literacy by collecting and distributing gently used books (currently some seventy thousand a year) to day care centers, schools, clinics, and homes.

Last year, when I was thinking about how to celebrate R.J. Julia's fifteenth birthday, it occurred to me that these two aspects of my experience as a bookseller—the difference I've seen books make in lives, and the need for books in all of our communities—could come together. We would ask authors who had appeared at the store to write about a book that changed their lives, not only to enjoy their stories, but as a reminder and a provocation that books do in fact change lives. I do think we need to be reminded that books are not some quaint, obsolete product, and who better than a group of wonderful writers to convey that message, to delight readers and inspire them to return to old favorites or seek out new treasures. Equally important, we would use such a book to bring more books to more children by donating the profits to Read to Grow.

In some Connecticut cities, and in many cities and towns across our country, the rate of functional illiteracy exceeds 70 percent. There is an undeniable correlation between functional illiteracy, poverty, and crime—in fact, eleven states predict their future need for prison cells based on the reading levels of their fourth graders. Books can change lives, yes, and so can the lack of them. It happens that the royalty on *The Book That Changed My Life*, for each copy sold, is just about equal to what Read to Grow pays for the new books it distributes, so your purchase of this book buys a book for a child.

As my mother knew so well, and as the seventy-one essays collected here testify so powerfully, putting the right book in the right hand can mean the world. I know this from my own experience, and I know it because I've seen the faces of children who have discovered the magic of reading, I've seen the faces of teenagers who have found comfort in a character or a story, I've seen the faces of adults who have learned to understand others in a different and enlightened way. Yet when I sat down recently with the final manuscript of *The Book That Changed My Life* and read it in one sitting, even I, who so firmly believe in the notion that books can change lives, was surprised and moved by the profound impact of books on the contributors. In *The Art of Possibility*, Rosamund Stone Zander and Benjamin Zander write that art "is about rearranging us, creating surprising juxtapositions, emotional openings, startling presences, flight paths to the eternal," and that's exactly what the contributors describe in their essays, each in a different and unique way. Apart from the sheer beauty of the essays, they are a dramatic reminder that everywhere, every day, someone is changed, perhaps even saved, by words and stories.

The Book That Changed My Life

The Bluest Eye

TONI MORRISON

DOROTHY ALLISON

I remember first the power of the language: "Here is the house. . . . Dick and Jane . . . the fall of 1941 . . . Nuns go by as quiet as lust. . . . Love, thick and dark as Alaga syrup," and yes, that child left "among the garbage and the sunflowers." And then I remember the girls: eleven-year-old Pecola Breedlove, of course, and the storyteller, Claudia, and her sister, Frieda, both younger than Pecola, nine and ten.

I remember the blue-and-white Shirley Temple cup from which Pecola drinks so much milk, as if it might turn her into Shirley herself—"old squint-eyed Shirley," as Claudia calls her. I loved that Claudia spoke that way, cursing that paragon of smug prettiness, contemptible and daunting at the same time. I read that line and laughed out loud. "Old squint-eyed Shirley." Is it possible to absorb a book so completely that you miss the fact that it is not about you and yours but about people so unlike you that you ignore all the ways they are different?

When Claudia looked with hate at little white girls, I took no offense. I thought instead about the way I had looked at those distant and horrible images of pretty, well-dressed, respectable little white girls held out as models for me and my sisters. It had been made perfectly clear to us that we would never be their equals—not us, with our ragged clothes, bad teeth, and shiftless ways. My sisters and I were not delicate loved creatures but workhorses, animal-strong and rough, and ready for roughness. But no child wants to be treated so badly. I wanted love as much as Claudia or Frieda or Pecola, and I identified with Claudia's angry resentments and her sharp judgment of those who damned her so easily. I knew, of course, I knew absolutely that Claudia was black and that *The Bluest Eye* was most of all about the hatred and contempt directed at little black girls, but in my white heart what rocked and shifted was my sense of the great contempt directed also at me and mine. I knew that the hatred thrown at Claudia was kin to the contempt thrown at us. Just as I knew that we had, in our white skin, a measure of privilege denied to Claudia, Frieda, and Pecola. There was this thing, racism, and there was no denying that we benefited from it. I had eyes, I could look around and see. But when I read *The Bluest Eye,* what I saw too was the common cause of hurt and self-hatred. And something more—something about the nature of love and forgiveness.

Can a book make such a difference? Can it change you utterly?

I know it can.

I read *The Bluest Eye* as a grown-up woman, but one who still carried within her the child she had been. And I read it like a prayer. I remember speaking the words on the pages out loud, that heartbreaking absolution: "The best hiding place was love." I remember looking up and thinking, This changes everything. I knew that family. It felt like my own, Claudia's family, her mother's rough and demanding and comforting hands. But also Pecola's family, her father's brutal use and oblivious ruthlessness. I had been used like that, had learned to hate myself for it, had put my lips to the cup of bitterness and rinsed my mouth with the liquor stink of self-hatred and shame.

It was not the subject matter, the language, the courage, or the simple beauty of the narrative. It was not that it was about poverty, incest, rape, violence, and hatred—and I had read nothing up to that moment that remade those horrors in the particular way Toni Morrison remade them on the page. It was not the bravery of taking up those subjects and naming them fit for narrative. Well, it was all that, of course, but it was more. It was the storyteller, Claudia, who looked at the world with unflinching honesty, the beauty and the ugliness alike. I understood her, the way she raked at her own soul, holding herself responsible for sins she should never have thought hers. Smart and stubborn and full of human hurt, Claudia is the narrator who retells everything that happened. She holds herself and her sister and her whole community responsible for the destruction of the soul of Pecola Breedlove, but in telling the story shows so clearly how wide and high that responsibility rises.

The Bluest Eye made it plain. The world could be different if truth was told in such gorgeous and stark ways.

I want to do that, I thought. Not, I can do that. I could not imagine a world in which I could put voice to all the things I thought and remembered and imagined about being poor and hated and used and denied. But oh lord, if I could, if I could make a story that would touch someone else's heart the way this one touched mine. If I could repay a tenth of what I owed this storyteller, this brave and wonderful woman on the page, I would give anything.

I would give anything—and will. This is a debt that passes to the reader—to take up the story and remake the world. It changed me utterly. It changes me still. It remade my life.

DOROTHY ALLISON is the author of two novels, *Bastard Out of Carolina,* a finalist for the 1992 National Book Award, and *Cavedweller,* a New York Times Notable Book of 1998. Her other works include *The Women Who Hate Me: Poetry 1980–1990; Trash,* a collection of short stories; *Two or Three Things I Know for Sure,* a memoir; and *Skin: Talking About Sex, Class and Literature.*

Pricksongs & Descants

ROBERT COOVER

KATE ATKINSON

I read my way through a solitary childhood. Books were the bedrock of my emotional and intellectual life, books that proscribed no limit to the imagination, books that were full of resourceful girls, princesses and goatherds and Victorian maidens, not to mention the sand fairies, the talking animals, the scheming stepfamilies, and the handsome men who had been transformed into beasts, both real and metaphorical. Fairy tales, in particular, fed my imagination when it was most hungry—so much peril, so many possibilities!

And then I put away childish things and "books" became "literature," something I studied rather than simply read. And it was magnificent, it was transcendental. It was the light at the end of Daisy's dock, it was the wind howling on the moors above Haworth, it was the *whale,* for God's sake. It nourished and challenged and smote, but it wasn't really what you would call fun (except perhaps for *Tristram Shandy*—and Nabokov). Then someone gave me a copy of Robert Coover's *Pricksongs & Descants*, and literature became a book again, a book with no boundaries.

"We need all the imagination we have, and we need it exercised and in good condition," Robert Scholes has written, and Coover exercised it in every possible way in this collection of stories—myths and allegories, multiplicities of viewpoints, parables, fairy stories, protean characters, protean narratives, parodies, ever-shifting texts of paranoia and terror and sex and death. There are characters who are aware that something has gone horribly awry with the story they find themselves in, narrators who are puzzled by their own narration. ("Wait a minute, this is getting out of hand!") There are stories that wrap around on themselves like a coiled snake or never get beyond the beginning. A box of ludic tricks and delights, a world where "anything can happen," as one omnipotent Prospero-like narrator declares. Oh, and a wonderful and mysterious obsession with doors. Doors of perception, doors of invention. Over the threshold and into the world of the imagination. For the first time I was reading the kind of book that I would have liked to write myself. (If only.) The fun was back and this time it was serious.

Coover led me to the writers who had been there all the time—Borges, Barth, Vonnegut, and onward to the wonderful world of Barthelme. (In the first edition of my own collection of stories, *Not the End of the World,* there is a misprint in the dedication of the last story. What should have read, "For Donald Barthelme, gone but living on in the words," actually reads, "For Donald Barthelme, living on in the woods." I like to think he would have appreciated the absurdity of that.)

Coover is particularly good at dazzling reworkings of the fairy tale, which is "the first tutor of children," Walter Benjamin writes, and "secretly lives on" in every story. In "The Door," Red Riding Hood approaches her fate, but really she could be every reader.

> Even as the sun suddenly snapped its bonds and jerked westward, propelling her over the threshold, she realized that though this was a comedy from which, once entered, you never returned, it nevertheless possessed its own astonishments and conjurings, its towers and closets, and even more pathways, more gardens, and more doors.

Barthelme and Coover were at the heart of my doctoral thesis on the "New Fiction" of the sixties and seventies in America, a thesis that was refused at the viva for all kinds of reasons now forgotten by everyone but me, but I suspect mostly because no one in my English department had heard of writers like Coover, Barthelme, Gass, Katz, Sukenick. They didn't conform, they weren't listening to the wind howling on the moors, they *were* the wind.

What I discovered, curiously, was that I had found my own sense of creativity in writing about other people's books, and when I was forcibly stopped, I was bereft for a while. I felt as though I had lost those writers and their writing, but that is impossible, of course, we carry all the writing inside us from the very first word. And then one day I woke up and wrote my first story. It wasn't much (as I recall, it began, "It is raining . . .") but it was a start. It opened a door.

KATE ATKINSON is the author of the novels *Case Histories*, *Emotionally Weird*, *Human Croquet*, and *Behind the Scenes at the Museum*, which was named Whitbread Book of the Year in 1995. She has also written a play, *Abandonment,* and a collection of short stories, *Not the End of the World*. She lives in Edinburgh.

Selected Poems

GWENDOLYN BROOKS

JAMES ATLAS

It was 1963, and I was fourteen, on a trip through Europe with my family. One day, exploring Paris on my own, I stumbled across the shrine known to every Parisian tourist for generations: Shakespeare and Company, the Left Bank bookshop in a tall narrow building just across from Notre Dame. I bought three books that day: *Dangling Man*, by Saul Bellow; a battered copy of *Studs Lonigan* (the first volume), by James T. Farrell; and *Selected Poems,* by Gwendolyn Brooks.

What did these books have in common? They were by Chicago writers. I had literary aspirations myself, and as a boy from Evanston, the town just north of Chicago, I was excited by the idea that writers existed there—contemporary writers, still productive and alive (and not even old, it would turn out), writers who proved that you didn't need to live in Paris or New York to be the real thing. They wrote in a recognizable idiom, urban, plainspoken, unsentimental. And the places they wrote about were familiar.

Joseph, Bellow's Dangling Man, lives in Hyde Park, on the South Side of Chicago; he hangs out in coffee shops, rides the elevated train, wanders the desolate wintry streets. This is the world he knows: "The giants of the last century had their Liverpools and Londons, their Lilles and Hamburgs to contend against, as we have our Chicagos and Detroits." Joseph belongs to a civilization too.

Farrell's novel, *Young Lonigan*, brought similar news from a different Chicago neighborhood: the Irish South Side. Studs Lonigan wasn't bookish; he wasn't a dreamy, sensitive boy like Bernard in *Passage from Home,* a novel about growing up in Chicago that I adored, by Bellow's friend Isaac Rosenfeld. Studs was a streetwise kid toughened by life in the tenements; he knew that it wouldn't be easy to make his way in the world. I admired his resilience.

The third book I carried to the cash register of Shakespeare and Company was Brooks's poems, the cover a primitive woodcut of flowers, black against a gray background. (My memory of more than forty years ago was confirmed when I ordered a copy from that marvelous Internet tool Abebooks, an online consortium that embraces the entire English-speaking world and enables you to buy *any* book secondhand, usually for just a few dollars.) Brooks also lived in Chicago—I knew very little else about her—and wrote about a different stratum of its rich culture: the Negroes (as they were then called) of Bronzeville, the vast black slums of the South Side. Brooks wrote in a formal voice, sonnets and quatrains and lyrics rich with literary echoes; but those forms contained within them the experience and idiom of the poverty-hardened neighborhoods that fascinated me from a distance: taverns, street fights, abortions, "the liquor of battle bleeding black air dying and demon noise." There was one poem, brief and terse, that I can still recite from memory.

We Real Cool

THE POOL PLAYERS.
SEVEN AT THE GOLDEN SHOVEL.

We real cool. We
Left school. We

Lurk late. We
Strike straight. We

Sing sin. We
Thin gin. We

Jazz June. We
Die soon.

What was it about this poem that thrilled me as I read it on a bench in the tiny park across the street from Shakespeare and Company? The singsong cadence, for one thing, with its ominous message, conveyed in the internal rhymes of the twenty-four one-syllable words that make up the poem. It brought back to me the image of a street scene, a knot of black guys loitering in front of a liquor store with iron gates, that I'd glimpsed driving through the South Side with my parents on the way to visit relatives in a western suburb. It was brittle, raw, authentic. More than the rhyme or meter was the *reality:* poetry could emerge out of the geography of your own experience, the life you lived or knew.

JAMES ATLAS is the author, most recently, of *Bellow: A Biography* and *My Life in the Middle Ages.* He is the founding editor of the Penguin Lives series, and now, as president of Atlas Books, publishes the Eminent Lives and Great Discoveries series.

The Power of Myth

JOSEPH CAMPBELL, WITH BILL MOYERS

ROBERT BALLARD

Books are so much a part of my life that it is hard to pick out a favorite, but if I had to, it would be *The Power of Myth*, Bill Moyers' collection of interviews with Joseph Campbell. So many aspects of their conversation found a home in my heart and soul. For instance, finding your "other half" is such a wonderful way of defining the relationship we should have with our mate in life.

But the interview I love most deals with our common journey in life, which Campbell states so simply: that life is the act of becoming, that you never arrive. That you climb your mountains not for the view you have once you reach the summit but because you love the process of climbing, of becoming.

For me, *The Power of Myth* reinforced my view that life is a series of journeys, circles within circles on which you travel through time and space and within yourself. Each journey begins with a dream that grows into a passion to do something important in life. That passion motivates you to learn, to prepare yourself to fulfill your dream. Finally, you begin the journey itself, which in my case commonly becomes an expedition to find something lost or unknown.

During that journey I know I will be tested by the storms we must all experience. Some storms will test your mental preparation, but the most challenging will test the strength of your passion and your willingness to endure those storms to reach your goal. And I have learned that all storms will pass: the skies clear, and your quest is achieved.

But your journey is never over until you return from it to share with society what you have learned. Then and only then can you begin your next journey in life as the process repeats itself, as you constantly become.

Among the most accomplished of the world's deep-sea explorers, ROBERT BALLARD is best known for his historic discovery of the RMS *Titanic.* During his long career, Dr. Ballard has conducted more than a hundred deep-sea expeditions. He is the author of bestselling books on his discovery of the *Titanic* and the *Bismarck*, and the recipient of many prestigious awards, including the Explorer's Club's Explorer's Medal, the National Geographic Society's Hubbard Medal, the Lindbergh Award, and the National Humanities Medal. He is an explorer in residence for the National Geographic Society, president of the Institute for Exploration, director of the newly created Institute for Archaeological Oceanography at the University of Rhode Island, and founder of the JASON Project, an award-winning educational program that reaches more than 1.7 million students and 38,000 teachers annually.

The Snake Has All the Lines

Jean Kerr

Gina Barreca

I have an intimate relationship with books. After all, I take them with me into the bathtub—not an invitation I offer lightly. The first book I ever took with me into the shower, however, was *The Snake Has All the Lines*, by Jean Kerr.

I was eight years old. The book was new. It was a mass-market paperback with colored page edges, and it belonged to my older brother. This fact sincerely bothered but in no way deterred me from sneaking it behind the opaque plastic curtain and turning on the water so I could read it undisturbed.

I couldn't put it down.

Most people use that phrase as a figure of speech. For me, it was not only literal but pathological: had someone attempted to remove *The Snake Has All the Lines* from my grubby hands, I would have shrieked as if my fingernails were being ripped out. Even though I was too young to get most of the jokes, I was so enthralled by this hysterically funny book that I made it mine by ruining it for anyone else. I let it get soaked, realizing that even if my brother wanted to read it, or my parents, for that matter, they would eschew a frankly tumescent tome. I'm not making a case for wrecking other people's valuables, mind you; I'm just highlighting the level of cunning to which I sank in order to possess Kerr's book. Which I did. I read it until the pages fell out—and once again I speak literally.

In a weird twist of fate, a girlfriend of one of my lesser cousins had given *The Snake Has All the Lines* to my brother as a present. Why she gave a thirteen-year-old boy a book of comic essays from the perspective of a middle-aged woman I'll never be able to fathom. It will be one great mystery to me, like the pyramids. I'm endlessly grateful to the nameless young woman who brought Jean Kerr into my life, though I will never understand why it happened. I just got lucky.

You'll want to know the origin of the title. The eldest of Kerr's six children returned home one day from his Catholic school and announced that he'd been cast as Adam in a play based on Genesis. "You're playing Adam? Why, that's wonderful, that's the *lead*!" applauds dutiful mother Kerr. "Yeah," her son says, "but the *snake* has all the lines." As a touchstone for Kerr's humor, the exchange is perfect. Willing to mix the pious and the profane, the big and little issues, the domestic and the existential, Kerr is the quintessential female humorist.

Okay, so I didn't have a theory of women's humor when I was eight years old, sitting on the edge of the tub as the shower's spray cooled, but the idea sank deeper than the water blotting the pages: what a terrific thing it would be to make people laugh. It wasn't lost on me either that Kerr decided to become a writer when she was eight years old. "I won't say there was a blinding flash," she writes of this epiphany, "but there was a sweet recognition of the moment of truth not unlike that memorable instant in which Johnny Weissmuller first noticed that he was Tarzan and not Jane."

How did Jean Kerr know she was destined to be an author? Because she didn't want to get up in the morning. By writing books, she could afford to hire someone else to do her chores. It sounded like the perfect plan to me, and I have tried to pattern my life's work along these inspirational lines.

GINA BARRECA, a professor of English at the University of Connecticut and an award-winning columnist for the *Hartford Courant*, is the author of *They Used to Call Me Snow White . . . but I Drifted*, *Perfect Husbands (And Other Fairy Tales)*, and *Babes in Boyland: A Personal History of Co-education in the Ivy League*, as well as the editor of *Don't Tell Mama!: The Penguin Book of Italian American Writing*, *The Signet Book of American Humor*, and *The Penguin Book of Women's Humor.*

The Works of Shakespeare

Nicholas A. Basbanes

One of my lingering regrets from childhood is the loss long ago of my first library card, a passkey to wonder acquired when I was a boy growing up in Lowell, Massachusetts, and worn to tatters by the time I was ten. Books have always mattered to me, but until my junior year at Bates College, when I took a two-semester course devoted entirely to the works of William Shakespeare, I was an English major, no more, no less, choosing that line of study because I loved to read and because I had always wanted to be a writer.

The great bard's thirty-eight plays, one hundred fifty-four sonnets, and assorted narrative poems came to us in that class by way of a stout one-volume edition from Scribner's with excellent introductions by Thomas Marc Parrott, but the realization that this weighty book might actually have an impact on my life did not arrive as a sudden epiphany, especially since I had read a good number of the works beforehand, and had a pretty good idea of what they were about. There was no eureka moment, in other words, when I said to myself, I am a richer person because of this, even though it became clear to me over time that this indeed was the case.

What happened, essentially, was that I fell under the spell of an extraordinary teacher by the name of Robert Berkelman (1900–1975), an English professor with a legendary reputation for crankiness, but one whose passion for Shakespeare was infectiously palpable, and whose knowledge of the canon was formidable. Professor Berkelman was eager to share, but he demanded your best in return. (He once opened a class with this challenge: "Keats did it before he was twenty-four. Could you?")

A principle Berkelman instilled in his students—that you could read the same text repeatedly over time, and that something fresh and new would declare itself with each reading—was a revelation to me. Not only did I learn to engage a text critically under his tutelage, I learned to savor the beauty of the written word in ways previously unimaginable to me, and to appreciate the power it has to transform lives. It is no exaggeration to report that I was totally dazzled by the imagery, the poetry, and the insights Shakespeare offered into the frailties of human nature. I can honestly say I entered adulthood during the turbulent 1960s with William Shakespeare by my side as guide, seer, and companion, and that he has been with me ever since.

Something else Professor Berkelman preached in all his courses—and I took eight with him over four years, quite possibly a Bates record—was the merit of reading favorite passages aloud, a practice I use to this day, most productively with my own writing. When my daughters were children in the 1980s, it became customary for us to read their literary assignments together at night, and to discuss what we had just learned as we went along. Shakespeare's plays were by far the most fun for us. We selected our roles, assumed what we thought were appropriate voices, and visualized the scenes as if we were directors staging our own productions. We tinkered with the blank verse, examined the language, shared our perceptions. Most of all, we allowed reading to enter our lives, and to work its magic.

NICHOLAS A. BASBANES has worked as an award-winning investigative reporter, a literary editor, and a nationally syndicated columnist. His first book, *A Gentle Madness: Bibliophiles,*

Bibliomanes, and the Eternal Passion for Books, was a finalist for the National Book Critics Circle Award in General Nonfiction for 1995, and was named a New York Times Notable Book of the Year. He is also the author of *Patience and Fortitude, A Splendor of Letters, Among the Gently Mad*, and *Every Book Its Reader: The Power of the Printed Word to Stir the World*. He is now working on a centennial history of Yale University Press.

The Lord of the Rings

J. R. R. Tolkien

Graeme Base

In this age of www.lordoftherings.com and countless other Web sites, games, spin-offs, and associated enterprises, it feels strangely uninspired, sheeplike almost, to confess that the book that did most to set my sails for the future, back in the early seventies, was J. R. R. Tolkien's massive tome *The Lord of the Rings.*

I was thirteen or thereabouts, into sport and music, not a reader beyond what was necessary for schoolwork. Books were at best a brief diversion, at worst a necessary evil. Reading for pleasure wasn't something I did or understood—not unusual for a thirteen-year-old boy. What I did do that was unusual, or at least would be unusual now, was learn Latin, which brought me into contact with a singular man with the striking name of Virgil J. Cain—my Latin teacher. As I look back on Virgil J. Cain from the distance of more than three decades, he strikes me still as more like J. R. R. Tolkien than anyone else I have ever met or am ever likely to meet. He looked like Tolkien, he wrote like Tolkien, he was a lover of languages like Tolkien, he smoked a pipe like Tolkien, and of course he knew and loved *The Lord of the Rings.*

My brother, two years older, was given the book first. He didn't do Latin, but he was also befriended by the language-loving, pipe-smoking Virgil J. Cain. As Patrick read, I picked up hints of the tale in advance and became, perhaps, just a little intrigued. Something about a ring, things called hobbits, . . . but 1,086 pages? Are you kidding?

I can't remember starting the book, but I can remember finishing it. I cried. How dare it come to an end? Only 1,086 pages? I wanted it to go on and on, not because I had escaped into another world—I had enough going on in my own to have no need of escape—but because I had been utterly captivated by the romance, the fantasy, the sheer epic enormity of the thing. More a prisoner than an escapee!

The book that changed my life? What had changed in me? Simply put, I finally got it: a book could do more than help you pass an exam, it could lift you up and sweep you away. And I liked the feeling.

Mervyn Peake's Gormenghast trilogy followed, recommended by my sister, and then a swag of fantasy and sci-fi, notably the works of Ursula Le Guin and Anne McCaffrey. Brother Patrick acted as a filter, as for many years he devoured sci-fi novels at an alarming rate. I read those he recommended, and there were lots. But after hundreds of other sweeping sagas, other captivating concepts, other weird and wonderful worlds, still *The Lord of the Rings* remained, and remains, the one that made me cry out, "It's not enough! It can't end! I want MORE!"

GRAEME BASE is the author and illustrator of *Animalia, The Eleventh Hour, The Water Hole, Jungle Drums*, and many other picture books widely acclaimed for their wit and lush detail. He lives in Melbourne with his artist wife and their three children.

The Little Engine That Could

I Think I Can

Jeff Benedict

"Let's read a book." When I was a little boy, that's what my mother used to say to me at bedtime. She read all sorts of children's books to me. We read my favorite ones—like *Mike Mulligan and His Steam Shovel* and *Where the Wild Things Are*—over and over, but the one we read most often was *The Little Engine That Could.* I can still remember the glossy feel of its pages and the colorful illustrations of trains, animals, toys, and candy.

Mostly, however, I remember the lessons my mother taught me from the story. One lesson was about humility. At the outset of the book, a train carrying toys to children breaks down. A shiny passenger train and a big locomotive each pass by the stranded toys that are pleading for deliverance. Although able, both trains feel too important to help. This arrogance ultimately hurts the children.

Service, my mother taught, has the opposite effect. It can replace a child's tears with a smile. My mother knew this from experience. She was a single mom. I was her only child. She worked hard, but money was tight. If not for the help of others, we would sometimes have gone without basics like groceries, clothing, and even housing. Maybe that's why she and I were so drawn to the Little Engine That Could. He came to the rescue.

Mother started calling me her Little Engine That Could.

"Look at this little train and look at what he can do," she would say. "You're my little boy and you're like this little engine."

Even when I became a teen, my mother would remind me of the Little Engine's motto whenever I began to doubt my abilities: *I think I can.* Over time, this phrase—short and simple—changed my life in a dramatic way. When I decided to become an author I had no writing experience. None. I had never written for a magazine or newspaper. I had not studied journalism in college. In fact, I had never even taken a writing course. I was a lot like the Little Engine that had no sense of the mountain's height when he promised to take the toys up over the top. I didn't know enough about publishing to know that starting out with a book is a very tall order. I just thought I could write one. And I did.

My confidence to try new things and be unafraid of failure began with a simple children's book. Besides the importance of humility, service, and self-confidence, *The Little Engine That Could* taught me the priceless value of taking time to read with children. Unbeknownst to me, my mother saved most of my favorite children's books, storing them in boxes. When I became a parent, she wrapped them up and gave them to me as a gift so that I could read them to my own children.

I am now the father of four. In the tradition of my mother, my wife and I read individually to them every night. As a result, they love books too. There is no greater tool for bonding with children than books. There is no greater instrument for teaching lessons for life. Now my children reach for books before they reach for the remote control. No doubt one day they will read to their children, a family tradition that started with *The Little Engine That Could.*

JEFF BENEDICT is an award-winning investigative journalist, a bestselling author of six books, and an attorney. He has been a contributing writer for *Sports Illustrated*, the *Los Angeles*

Times, and the *Hartford Courant*. His subjects have included Indian casinos, the Kobe Bryant case, forensic science, crime, addiction, political corruption, popular culture, and violence against women. He is also a frequent television news commentator and an essayist whose work has appeared in *The New York Times*, *The Chronicle of Higher Education*, and ESPN's online magazine. Benedict and his wife, Lydia, are the parents of four children. They reside in Connecticut.

The Catcher in the Rye

J. D. Salinger

The Book That Made Me a Writer

Elizabeth Berg

Winter, 1964. I'm sitting in my eleventh-grade English class with my hand up. When Mrs. Yeatman (not her real name, as at age fifty-six I'm just as frightened of her as I was at age sixteen) calls on me, I say, "Excuse me, but why do we have to memorize Chaucer's prologue to *The Canterbury Tales* in Middle English?"

"Because I say so," she says. She wears black cat-eye glasses and a lacquered beehive. Her posture is ramrod straight. She tucks her blouses tightly into her skirt, and her buttons are buttoned all the way up, and the sleeves of her cardigan are all the way down. Her jewelry? A watch. Undoubtedly with the time set according to the U.S. Naval Observatory Master Clock. I draw in a breath and persist. "I just don't see what *good* it's going to do us." She smiles. Sort of. About a week later, when it's my turn, I stand up and dutifully recite, "Whan that Aprill with his shoures soote . . ."

Spring, 1966. I'm the only one in Mrs. Yeatman's advanced class (I excel in English), because everyone else has gone to the National Honor Society meeting (I excel in indifference to other subjects). So it's just me and the terrifying Her Stiffness. I doodle in a notebook. Then I write something about a tree in a forest, but really I'm writing about myself. When I've finished,

I raise my hand. I know. You can imagine how foolish I felt, being the only one in the classroom and raising my hand. But it was Mrs. *Yeatman*. You didn't just speak out. You didn't say, "Yo, Claire!" You raised your hand and cleared your throat. Quietly.

For her part, she raised her eyebrows, arched perfectly, with nary a trace of vulgar eyebrow pencil.

"Can I show you something?" I asked. "*May* I."

She nodded, and I approached her desk, which felt like approaching the starship *Enterprise*. I handed her my notebook. She read my words, hesitated, looked up and said, "Hmph. Very good." And there was something in her eyes. Not admiration. Not a twinkle, not from Mrs. Yeatman. But a kind of connection, a little "Yes. I know." And from that connection came a direction that, for me, was right. Was true.

That moment is what began my career in publishing, because it was the first time I offered up something of my own, in my own way, to a reader and critic. Never mind that it took years before I did the real thing and sent a piece to a magazine. From then on, I had my style, my voice. I'd come to it from reading *The Catcher in the Rye*.

That book was not assigned by Mrs. Yeatman. Of course it wasn't assigned by Mrs. Yeatman; *Beowulf* was assigned by Mrs. Yeatman. No, I read J. D. Salinger because I'd heard about *The Catcher in the Rye*. What I'd heard was that it was dirty. My friend Donna, who'd transferred to our lame school after being kicked out of her fancy private one, said no, *Catcher* was *good* is what it was; it was *great*. I thought, Well, let's see. I opened the book and read the first sentence and thought, *Huh?* And then I devoured the book and when I was finished I went right back to the first page and started over again. I kept thinking, I didn't know you could do this! I didn't know you could write this way! It was so open. So close to the bone. So conversational. *Catcher in the Rye* showed me that you could write "to" someone you'd never met as if you were talking to someone you'd always known. That you could tell a secret publicly and it would still be a secret privately. That you could reveal the most profound emotions in the simplest of language, that in fact it was more effective to do it like that because then the writer got out of the reader's way. It taught me that the smallest of gestures could reveal all you needed to know about a character. That humor and pain could exist on the page beside each other, if not *in*side each other.

I couldn't sit still after I read that book. It was the literary aphrodisiac to end all literary aphrodisiacs. I began writing in earnest, and I haven't slowed down yet.

It's obvious, I hope, that I don't mean to compare myself to J. D. Salinger. I don't think anyone's ever come close to what Salinger did in *The Catcher in the Rye*—there's only one book like it—but the writers inspired by it must be countless. I'm a grateful one of them.

ELIZABETH BERG is the bestselling author of fourteen novels, among them *The Year of Pleasures, The Art of Mending, Joy School, Open House, Say When, Durable Goods, Range of Motion,* and *Talk Before Sleep.* The winner of the New England Book Award for her body of work, she is also the author of a story collection, *Ordinary Life*, and a book of nonfiction, *Escaping into the Open: The Art of Writing True.* She lives in Chicago.

The Most of P. G. Wodehouse

P. G. Wodehouse

Amy Bloom

I could say that the book that changed my life was *Pride and Prejudice.* It certainly introduced me to the terrible, seductive intersection of romance and commerce, and I took to beginning conversations at school with "It is universally acknowledged that . . ." Jane Austen opened my eyes, improved my diction, and left me isolated on the playground at Arrandale Elementary. Dickens did the same with *A Tale of Two Cities.* I wept for Sydney Carton, my secret self, and all the other marvelous, brave, misunderstood aristocrats, and if that's what got in the way of my family's socialist past and my Weatherman future, it may have been for the best. *Catcher in the Rye* spoke to me, frank and wounded and funny, as nothing else had, and Dorothy Parker gave me hope that bitter wit and striking looks could take a girl further than a soft nature and blond curls.

I found all these books on my father's bookshelves, which included the classics and his particular postwar favorites: S. J. Perelman; Parker; Robert Benchley; the wonderful and disturbing James Thurber; fey, droll Saki; and John Collier, whose *Fancies and Goodnights* I still pursue every time I'm in a used bookstore. I read them all, all the time, and for my father and me, my lying on the floor not too far from his armchair, reading his favorite books, was as good as our relationship was likely to get. Conversation that touched on our real lives—my intransigence, his pomposity, my recklessness, his opprobrium—ruined everything.

P. G. Wodehouse made my father laugh out loud. And then he would hand me the book and point to the page, tears in his eyes, and I would read the page and a few pages more until he took the book back, and I would laugh until I fell down on the living room rug.

> He might be in the soup, he might be a financial wreck, he might be faced with a *tête-à-tête* with his uncle, Lord Blicester, in the course of which the testy old man would in all probability endeavor to bite a piece out of the fleshy part of his leg, but at least he had done the fine, square thing. ("Noblesse Oblige")

> . . . I had got it into my head that the first thing thrown at Tuppy would be a potato. One gets these fancies. It was, however, as a matter of fact, a banana, and I saw in an instant that the choice had been made by wiser heads than mine. These blokes who have grown up from childhood in the knowledge of how to treat a dramatic entertainment that doesn't please them are aware by a sort of instinct just what is best to do, and the moment I saw that banana splash on Tuppy's shirt front I realized how infinitely more effective and artistic it was than any potato could have been.
>
> Not that the potato school of thought had not also its supporters. As the proceedings warmed up I noticed several intelligent-looking fellows who threw nothing else. ("Jeeves and the Song of Songs")

Either you find all of this, as Bertie Wooster would say, shatteringly funny, or you don't. I did, and my father did, and it marked me for life. I am a woman, a Jew, and a feminist—none of which would be admitted for even an afternoon to Bertie Wooster's Drones Club—and yet I love the Drones, for their cluelessness or ruthlessness or recklessness or whatever shocking deficits they display, predictably and hilariously. And despite my innate preference for the punchy one-liner, the clever, tough, urbane Lenny Bruce / Groucho Marx / Nichols and May humor, I am permanently in thrall to the dry, sweet drollery of Pelham Grenville Wodehouse. It is, as he would have said, an affliction of a certain, not unpleasant kind.

AMY BLOOM is the author of a novel, *Love Invents Us*, and two collections of stories: *Come to Me*, a finalist for the National Book Award, and *A Blind Man Can See How Much I Love You*, a finalist for the National Book Critics Circle Award. Her work has appeared in *The Best American Short Stories*, *The O. Henry Prize Short Stories*, *The New Yorker*, *The New York Times Magazine*, *Tin House*, *The Atlantic Monthly*, *Vogue*, *Slate*, and *Salon*, among other publications. She has also published a book of nonfiction, *Normal: Transsexual CEOs, Crossdressing Cops, and Hermaphrodites with Attitude.* She teaches writing at Yale University and is at work on a second novel, *Away*.

Little, Big

John Crowley

Harold Bloom

As I am now seventy-five and still a nonstop reader, I cannot nominate any single book as the one that changed my life. If only one, it would have to be the complete Shakespeare, with the Hebrew Bible a near rival, and a group of poets hovering not far away: John Milton, William Blake, Walt Whitman, Hart Crane, Wallace Stevens, Percy Bysshe Shelley, William Butler Yeats, Emily Dickinson, Robert Browning, among others.

But I have written extensively about everything so far mentioned, and desire to recommend strongly a fantasy novel much too little known, though it was first published a quarter century ago, John Crowley's *Little, Big* (1981). I have read and reread *Little, Big* at least a dozen times, and always am startled and refreshed. It seems to me the best book of its kind since Lewis Carroll's *Alice in Wonderland* and *Through the Looking Glass.* Like the Alice books, *Little, Big* is an imaginative masterpiece, in which the sense of wonder never subsides.

Little, Big is a family saga in which several generations live on surprisingly close terms with the faery folk, hence the title. So perpetually fresh is this book, changing each time I reread it, that I find it virtually impossible to describe, and scarcely can summarize it. I pick it up again at odd moments, sometimes when I wake up at night and can't fall back asleep. Though it is a good-sized volume, I think I remember every page. *Little, Big* is for readers from nine to ninety, because it naturalizes and renders domestic the marvelous.

Wallace Stevens said that poetry was "one of the enlargements of life." So is *Little, Big.* I have recommended it to scores of friends and students, and invariably they tell me they have found wisdom and delight.

HAROLD BLOOM, Sterling Professor of Humanities at Yale University and a former Charles Eliot Norton Professor at Harvard, is the author of more than twenty-five books, including *Jesus and Yahweh: The Names Divine*; *Where Shall Wisdom Be Found?*; *How to Read and Why*; *Shakespeare: The Invention of the Human*; *The Western Canon*; *The Book of J*; and *The Anxiety of Influence.* He is a MacArthur Prize Fellow, a member of the American Academy of Arts and Letters, and the recipient of the academy's Gold Medal for Belles Lettres and Criticism, among many other awards and honors.

Hiroshima

JOHN HERSEY

LARY BLOOM

Avoid Mr. Hill. This was the advice a senior gave to me and other eleventh graders who sought a less rigorous path to college.

But by the luck of the draw, in the fall of 1960, I found myself in Edwin Hill's English class. He looked out over his students—sons and daughters of Italian immigrants and of working-class Jews whose families had fled Cleveland proper for a suburb of new bungalows and all-white schools. We were earnest, well behaved, and, with a few dazzling exceptions, Midwest-ignorant. I had intentions of becoming a newspaper reporter but was fearful that someone like Mr. Hill would judge my work harshly and scribble in the margin, "You want to be a writer? Don't make me laugh."

Among the books on his reading list was John Hersey's *Hiroshima*, which I thought might interest me. My father had served in the Pacific. I had no idea that Hersey's account of the first atomic bomb blast on a city had already been printed in *The New Yorker* magazine. I had never heard of *The New Yorker.* Nor did I suspect that his book would immerse me in two wars.

As a boy, I was not a voracious reader, though at thirteen I had been so affected by Joseph and Stewart Alsop's *The Reporter's Trade* that I decided then and there what I wanted to do for a living. If the Alsop brothers taught the art of reporting, Hersey showed the reason for it. It was as a journalist that he breathed the radiated air of a devastated city to re-create the lives of men and women on the morning of August 6, 1945—people who were reading the newspaper or starting their workday or beginning their chores. This was a revelation. Hersey showed me the way to raise the stakes in writing—to avoid the shorthand of tragedy by carefully painting scenes with ordinary human beings.

I began my book report on *Hiroshima* with a sonnet I composed for the occasion. Why I did this I do not know, but it must have made an impression. At the next school open house, Mr. Hill told my parents that one day I might indeed be a writer.

What he couldn't foresee was this: I went to the Vietnam War. Though much of America couldn't fathom the reasons for involving our young soldiers, I could. Not that I was eager to go, but I believed our government's line about the besieged citizens of South Vietnam. Hersey's book had taught the oneness of humanity. I was not experienced enough then to know that our government's line was conceived in lies. All I knew was that those who were different from me—the kind of people we never saw in Mr. Hill's class or in our suburb—were nevertheless human beings. And that they were asking for our help. So off I went, not understanding that it was the last thing John Hersey would have wanted me to do.

LARY BLOOM is the author of *The Writer Within*, *Something Personal*, *Lary Bloom's Connecticut Notebook*, and *When the Game Is on the Line* (cowritten with Rick Horrow). He is also a playwright, lyricist, editor, and memoir teacher. He lives in Chester, Connecticut. His Web site is www.larybloom.net.

Expensive People

JOYCE CAROL OATES

and more

CHRIS BOHJALIAN

There really wasn't one book that changed my life. There was a stack of them.

When I was thirteen, my family moved from a suburb of New York City to Miami, Florida, and we moved there the Friday before Labor Day weekend. I started school the following Tuesday, and that afternoon I went to see my new orthodontist—a sadist, it would turn out, if ever there was one. He gave me some orthodontic headgear that looked like the business end of a backhoe, and I had to wear the apparatus for four hours a day when I was awake. I certainly wasn't about to sport it at school, given that immortality as the biggest geek ever to set foot inside Hialeah–Miami Lakes High wasn't chief among my aspirations. So I waited till school was over, and then my headgear and I went to the public library . . . and I read.

I read some of Stephen King's predecessors, since King was just starting to publish his impressive Grand Guignol. I read William Peter Blatty's *The Exorcist,* Peter Benchley's *Jaws*, and Thomas Tryon's deceptively fine novel *Harvest Home.* That autumn I also read Harper Lee's *To Kill a Mockingbird* and Joyce Carol Oates's *Expensive People.*

Remember the first line from *Expensive People*? "I was a child murderer." The opening paragraphs then deconstruct that short, cryptic sentence. Will the narrator prove to be a child who committed a murder or an adult who murdered a child?

I read those books in the library as well as in the den in our new home, and from them I learned a great deal that would help me as a writer. I learned the importance of linear momentum in plot from Blatty and Benchley and Tryon. I learned the importance of voice—and the role of person in fiction—from Lee and Oates. And I learned on a level that may not yet have been fully concrete, but that did indeed adhere, that the narrator in a first-person novel is a character too, and every bit as made-up as the fictional constructs around him or her.

Best of all, I learned of the comfort that can be taken from the pages of a book, and the friendship that can be found in a story.

CHRIS BOHJALIAN is the bestselling author of ten novels, including *Midwives*, *Before You Know Kindness*, *The Buffalo Soldier*, and *The Double Bind*, which will be published this winter. For more information, visit www.chrisbohjalian.com.

The Making of the President, 1960

THEODORE H. WHITE

STEVEN BRILL

When I was twelve years old, I somehow got hold of Theodore White's *The Making of the President, 1960*, the first of what was to become his series of groundbreaking inside reports on the presidential campaigns of the 1960s and 1970s. Although I was a bit younger than Teddy White's intended audience, I was fascinated with politics and I worshipped Kennedy. So, I loved White's narrative. I loved the intrigues and the personalities and the backroom dealings. I loved the idea that a reporter could get inside and tell us all that stuff. So much so that I handwrote a letter to Mr. White in care of his publisher. I guess 1962 was before publishing houses had PR handlers who vetted the letters sent to authors, because two weeks later I got back a similarly handwritten note (I still remember the thick blue ink) from White, scrawled at the bottom of my letter, thanking me for writing him and telling me how thrilled he was to have reached someone my age.

White's book—and his reply to my letter—made me want to be a writer who got inside big events and big institutions. And he made me try always to turn that reporting into a narrative.

STEVEN BRILL is the author of *Teamsters,* a bestselling book about the powerful union, and of *After,* which he wrote while working as a *Newsweek* columnist on all issues related to the aftermath of the September 11 attacks, and as a consultant to NBC on the same subject. A graduate of Yale College and Yale Law School, he is the founder and CEO of Verified Identity Pass, a system that expedites airport security screenings for members. He also founded *The American Lawyer* magazine, and created Court TV in 1991. He has written for *New York*, *Harper's*, and *Esquire*, among other publications, and teaches a seminar for aspiring journalists at Yale College.

The Denial of Death

ERNEST BECKER

BENJAMIN CHEEVER

When a friend sticks a book in my hand and crows, "It changed my life," my heart plummets. They never *say*, "It changed my life." They sing it out, as if boasting about intellectual suppleness, while not talking about the book at all. As if change were easy, welcome.

I know better. Sure, the Renaissance was change, but so was the Ice Age.

Plus, I'm not intellectually supple. When one of those books does come along, it knocks me over. I'll read it twice. If I can possibly get a recording of the book, I'll do so. I'll run with it in my iPod, wash the dishes with it. I'll dog-ear and underline my copy. I'll quote endlessly from the text in e-mail. I'll bore my neighbors, embarrass my friends, infuriate my family.

Sometimes it's a novel, sometimes a book of poetry. This year Ernest Becker's *The Denial of Death* has got me by the throat. Blackstone offers an excellent recording. "This book is a bid for the peace of my scholarly soul," Becker says in the preface.

He writes like Muhammad Ali used to boast, with a wild abandon that at first alienates and ultimately charms. "What does it mean to be a *self-conscious animal*? The idea is ludicrous, if it is not monstrous. It means to know that one is food for worms. This is the terror: to have emerged from nothing, to have a name, consciousness of self, deep inner feelings, an excruciating inner yearning for life and self-expression—and with all this yet to die."

Published in 1973, Becker's book is still a revelation in my little world. I particularly cherish his brilliant exposition—credited to Kierkegaard—on the vanity of sorrow. What a view! I'd never seen the world that way. This book changed my life. Argghh!!

BENJAMIN CHEEVER's most recent book of nonfiction, *Selling Ben Cheever*, was excerpted in *The New Yorker*, *Gourmet*, and *The New York Times Book Review.* His last novel, *The Good Nanny*, was selected as a New and Notable book by *The New York Times Book Review.* He was a reporter for a daily newspaper for six years and an editor at *Reader's Digest* for eleven, and has taught at Bennington College and the New School for Social Research. He's now writing *Strides*, a book about running, to be published by Rodale.

The Count of Monte Cristo

ALEXANDRE DUMAS

DA CHEN

Growing up poor in China during the seventies, I would do anything for a good meal, but I would do even more for a book. Books were a luxury that we often had to hand-copy. Ironic that I should love to read in the book desert China was then.

I wanted to read because I was a storyteller even as a little lad. A storyteller was essential in our village, which didn't have electricity. There were no movies, no malls (not that malls are any substitute for books), no television. When the sun set, only the moon was supposed to shine in our village. We had a fortune-teller who would sit under a pine tree every summer night, telling and retelling tales of love and hate, war and ghosts, that had been handed down for generations. We called him Mothman because he seemed to attract all the moths. (He got all the mosquitoes as well, I might add.) The entire village would be there after a day's hot labor in the scorching fields. Mothers would be dozing off, breast-feeding infants who sucked absentmindedly on their nipples. Fathers would be smoking long pipes, letting the old man's tales wash away their fatigue. I would sit right next to him, fanning him to keep his flow of story going. How I wished I were that old man.

Soon I became the Mothman of my generation. After school every day I would gather my followers. We would all climb up the same tree, hanging in the branches like monkeys, and I would tell the stories I had heard from the real Mothman. My listeners would rub my shoulders, scratch my back, and even light my cigarette to keep my story going.

Finally the day came when I ran out of stories and my listeners stopped coming. It was time to hit the bookstore or library. But all libraries were sealed during the Cultural Revolution; Mao forbade us to read any literature except works written by him. And there was no bookstore to speak of; such a little village did not deserve one in the eyes of the authorities.

One rainy day a buddy of mine came to my window shouting that a new bookstore had opened at the edge of our muddy village. We rushed off, splashing our way to the store, only to be told that we needed one fen, a Chinese penny, to rent one picture book to read in one sitting. An old convict who had returned from his twenty-year jail term manned the store. He had stolen two big sacks of rare forbidden books from an army library on the eve of his departure—not reformed at all.

We were so poor that we could not even afford one fen. Dad, working day and night, was barely able to feed us with yams. Mom cut our hair to save money to buy soy sauce. One day I spotted someone selling his used toothpaste tube to the commune's recycling store. He sold it for a fen, the exact amount needed to rent a book for one good read. The very next morning, I brushed my teeth five times, each time squeezing a fat worm of toothpaste onto my brush. When my mother looked at me suspiciously, I mumbled that I intended to intensify my dental care from that day on. She half believed me—my gums were all swollen. Within three days, I'd used up the entire toothpaste that Mother had bought for fifteen fen. I sold the aluminum tube for a fen and raced to the store to rent my first book.

The ex-convict wasn't very friendly. He stared at me the whole time I was there, reminding me not to damage the pages, those precious pages, by turning them too hastily. The picture book I picked was about a young Frenchman imprisoned in a dungeon though he had done no wrong. Within minutes, I was sucked into the book so completely that I forgot about the dreary drizzle of that Saturday afternoon. I forgot where I was and I became that French boy. I suffered with him in that darkness of hopelessness. Napoleon became my emperor. I flew away from myself and the little village I was trapped in.

The book was *The Count of Monte Cristo*, and it became the inspiration for my recent novel for young readers, *Wandering Warrior.*

Though the bookstore thrived on the pennies we village children scraped together by whatever means available—selling more used toothpaste tubes, digging rare herbs to sell to our commune's hospital, searching dusty corners of our fathers' drawers for misplaced change, collecting dried dog manure for fertilizer—it did not survive long. One day a few weeks after it opened, my buddy screamed hysterically through our window, "The bookstore is on fire!"

We rushed among the unhurried water buffalo, loosed from their plowing duties, toward the village corner where the store stood. The thatched roof of the hut was a ball of fire spewing a plume of dark smoke into the azure sky. We got so close to the hut that we could feel the heat pinching our skin. The store owner, usually an abrupt and arrogant man, was reduced to a pitiful sight. He was sobbing bitterly, trying to run back into the fire to salvage his precious books, and screaming something about wanting to be burned alive with them. Kind villagers restrained him and tried to comfort him.

The fire soon consumed the entire hut. Ashes were falling from the sky like dark snowflakes. I reached out and caught some in my palms. Those ashes contained the magical words that had touched our young hearts and lifted our souls. But gone were the books—oh, those windows of the world that had given us a glimpse of life beyond the narrow confines of our village existence. Then, in one brief second, the ashes were blown away by a quickening sea breeze.

The arsonist was none other than the party secretary of our commune, who had feared that the books were corrupting our young minds. He and the other Communist officials had wanted to burn the owner as well and had locked the doors from outside, but the ex-convict managed to escape through the window.

The party secretary took the books away from us, but not the seeds those fine books had sown. The deprivation didn't stop our thirst for books, it only heightened it. Whenever there was a book in circulation among the villagers, we would rip it apart and hand-copy each chapter, and within days a new book would exist. We roamed bigger villages and broke into sealed libraries so we could "borrow" books soaked in muck and overgrown with mold as a result of typhoon storms. Oh, even a moldy book smelled heavenly.

Years later, after I got my law degree from Columbia University and was working in a Wall Street investment bank, I decided to write about my childhood, the childhood of deprivation and dreams—more deprivation breeds more dreams. One of my silent dreams was to write books so no one could take them away from me. To write books so another village boy somewhere in the dark corners of the earth could subsist upon them, finding rays of hope and a glimpse of a future.

After nine months of writing in my spare time, my first memoir, *Colors of the Mountain*, came to be. With the blessing that could only come from above, the book was won by Random House chief Ann Godoff in an intense five-house auction, and was published to critical acclaim and commercial success. My second memoir, *Sounds of the River*, was published two years later, to be followed by *Wandering Warrior*, which was described by *USA Today* as a cross between Harry Potter and *Crouching Tiger, Hidden Dragon*.

Writers write for various reasons. I write because my heart demands so. There is such freedom in the simple act of sitting there, holding up my hands, waiting to pound on the computer keyboard, waiting for words to pour from the tips of my fingers and compose the melody of life from the faded tapestry of my past. That craving for freedom came from a deep princedom in my childhood, where a book was gold and a dream was but to hold it in your lap on a dreary Saturday afternoon, in that forgotten village far away, near the end of this earth.

DA CHEN is the bestselling author of the memoirs *Colors of the Mountain* and *Sounds of the River.* His first adult novel, *Brothers*, has just been published by Crown/Shaye Areheart Books. For more information, visit www.dachen.org.

Ida

Gertrude Stein

Saved by Ida-Ida

Harriet Scott Chessman

> There was a baby born named Ida. Its mother held it with her hands to keep Ida from being born but when the time came Ida came. And as Ida came, with her came her twin, so there she was Ida-Ida.

I stood in the Yale Co-op, in New Haven, Connecticut, one spring more than twenty years ago, and fell kite-high in love with this opening. I soon fell in love too with the feckless, quizzical character Ida and her twinning creator, Gertrude Stein.

I had never read a novel like *Ida,* so experimental, such a surprisingly giddy ride. Ida's life catapulted me back to my own childhood, when I'd known how books really *could* change the world through the sheer force of imagination. Her story resembles one a highly fierce and intelligent child might make up—or a writer who has the remarkable gift of holding on to the vision and feelings of childhood. It is this gift, I think, that is at the heart of any art that has the power to move us.

Ida's story, as I discovered that day in the Co-op, marveling over page after page, is absurd and moving, childlike and intellectually engaging, filled with details and habits that still delight me and make me laugh. In Ida's confusing and often frightening world, where people jump out of bushes, or disappear without explanation, or change into someone else entirely, she is a skilled creator of boundaries defining and protecting her "I" from those bent on pinning her with their own definitions. "Ida always hesitated before eating. That was Ida." And (one of my favorites): "She did not love anybody in Ohio." Naturally, "she always just had to have Tuesday. Tuesday was Tuesday to her." What Ida loves most is the essence of what any writer cherishes: "She liked to talk and to sing songs and she liked to change places." What she has to resist is beauty contests, and blandishments, and other people who claim to know her.

As I stood in the Co-op, a young faculty member and a new mother, worried about writing my first scholarly book in a highly competitive academic world, all I could think was, How did Stein *do* this? How did she have the courage? I hadn't yet read much of her earlier writing, even more experimental and wild in its playfulness with language, its way of turning words and stories and poems and plays inside out and upside down. All I knew was that Stein had said, "Rose is a rose is a rose," and I had no idea that such roses had anything to do with Emerson, or William James, or arising, or arousal, or love, or the beauty and freshness of language, or the desire to break through words into something real. I just opened myself to this spirited Ida who marries one "officer" after another, and who loses herself sometimes in the process—who vanishes from her own book at one especially low point—yet who rises gradually above the conventions of heterosexual marriage and politics and contests of all sorts in her search for her particular "genius," and for her "Andrew," a significant other, or "and," who can talk and listen to Ida just as her imaginary twin once did.

I loved this striking book for the courage it gave me to start looking for my own "genius," my own spirit, and my own writing life. Stein's influence was slow but profound. I can see now how her Ida offered me a ticket *out*. In writing my first book, about Stein's language of the body, I slowly learned how to hold on to my identity, to listen to myself and not to officers of any shape or description. Gertrude Stein showed me how to start honoring and embracing the Id, the idea, the "I," the soul, that came first, inside me. To write, as I know now, *is* to have a twin, to become Ida-Ida, to be constantly in dialogue with oneself and others in a way that is fruitful and always changing. It is a continuing birth, worthy of celebration.

HARRIET SCOTT CHESSMAN is the author of the novels *Someone Not Really Her Mother*, *Lydia Cassatt Reading the Morning Paper*, and *Ohio Angels*, as well as a scholarly book about Gertrude Stein, *The Public Is Invited to Dance.* Formerly associate professor of English at Yale University, she has also taught writing and literature at Bread Loaf School of English. A great fan of R.J. Julia Booksellers, she lived in Madison, Connecticut, for many years and now lives in the Bay Area, where she is at work on her fourth novel.

The Seven Storey Mountain

THOMAS MERTON

BROTHER CHRISTOPHER

There is a Greek word for time—*kairos*—which has a different sense than the ordinary passing of moments, the position of the hands on a clock. *Kairos* means a particular hour, a critical moment which, when it dawns, demands a decision from us.

Years ago I was studying in the School of Foreign Service at Georgetown University, planning for some sort of career in international affairs. It seemed like a decent plan at the time. My grades were good, and people I respected had assured me that I'd find the foreign service challenging and interesting. My life path seemed to be taking shape.

We never anticipate being changed by what we read. Such an experience cannot be planned for. To that point in my life, I had never read a book that I could say changed me. To be sure, I loved to read and had read widely, but my reading was more a form of entertainment than a transformative engagement. I was always detached from the book, on the outside looking in. All this changed in the span of a few short days.

Georgetown required its students to take several courses in theology and philosophy, and I was fulfilling part of that requirement with a course called Ways of Spirit and Desire, taught by Father Thomas King, a brilliant Jesuit. One of the books he assigned was *The Seven Storey Mountain*, the autobiography of the twentieth-century Trappist monk Thomas Merton.

I had no idea what I was walking into. From the first words, to paragraphs that moved beyond themselves effortlessly into chapter after chapter, I forgot that I was reading. I was too absorbed, swept into the story of how a young bohemian intellectual full of passion and fire gradually found his way to becoming a monk, entering a Trappist monastery in Kentucky at the age of twenty-six. How odd the tale was, and yet so utterly honest and understandable. Never before had words been so intimate to my own latent feelings, and never before had their honesty and authenticity moved me so deeply. Merton's journey charted a path into my own heart, stirring questions I did not dare ignore. Indeed, as I finished the book I felt an aliveness I had never known. *The Seven Storey Mountain* had awakened a primal desire that would henceforth be a factor in every decision I would ever make, in every moment of self-discovery I would ever experience.

Now, thirty years after the fact, from the perspective of a monastic calling that has unfolded in a life of communion—with God, my brothers and sisters, and the natural world around me—I am still surprised at its newness. Words cannot convey my gratitude.

BROTHER CHRISTOPHER was born in 1954 and grew up in the Chicago area. He graduated from college in 1977 with a B.A. in philosophy and immediately entered monastic life, being tonsured at New Skete in 1983. Throughout his years at New Skete he has been responsible for the dog-training program, and he was ordained a priest for the community in 1995. He has written several of the dog books the community is known for, and was the principal author of *In the Spirit of Happiness*, the community's book on the spiritual life, and *Rise Up*, a book of meditations.

A Stranger Is Watching

MARY HIGGINS CLARK

CAROL HIGGINS CLARK

From the time I learned to read in the first grade (which seems late these days!), I have always loved curling up with a book. The adventures of Jean, John, and Judy in my first parochial school reader whetted my appetite for the wonderful world of books. But it was when I was in college that I read the book that would change my life—and the book wasn't even finished yet!

It was the summer after my freshman year at Mount Holyoke College. My mother, Mary Higgins Clark, was writing her second suspense novel, *A Stranger Is Watching.* Her agent was anxiously awaiting the first one hundred pages. They were written, but they needed to be retyped, and those were the days before computers. My mother still had a nine-to-five job and was pressed for time. I volunteered to help.

While my mother was at work in New York City, I sat down at our kitchen table in New Jersey, the electric typewriter in front of me. I rolled a piece of paper into the machine and began retyping those pages, occasionally slowed as I tried to decipher my mother's handwritten inserts. But I loved the whole process. When my mother returned home, I discussed with her the plot, the characters, what she planned to do next. I couldn't wait for her to finish.

It was intriguing for me to see how the book took shape over time. When *A Stranger Is Watching* was published three years later, in 1978, it was a thrill finally to see it in print. As Jean,

John, and Judy had introduced me to the world of reading, retyping *Stranger* had introduced me to the wonderful, creative, sometimes frustrating world of a writer. It's why I became a writer. And that certainly changed my life.

All I can say is, I'm so glad computers weren't around back then!

CAROL HIGGINS CLARK is the author of nine bestselling Regan Reilly mysteries, including *Decked* (nominated for the Agatha and Anthony awards for Best First Novel), *Iced*, *Jinxed*, *Popped*, *Burned*, and most recently *Hitched*. She is coauthor, along with her mother, Mary Higgins Clark, of a bestselling holiday mystery series. Also an actress, Carol studied at the Beverly Hills Playhouse and has recorded several of her mother's works as well as her own novels. She received the AudioFile Earphones Award of Excellence for her reading of *Jinxed*. She lives in New York City, and her Web site is www.carolhigginsclark.com.

The Yearling

MARJORIE KINNAN RAWLINGS

Lolita

VLADIMIR NABOKOV

BILLY COLLINS

The opportunity to single out a book that "changed my life" makes me realize that no book leaves us unchanged, for better or worse. Why read otherwise? Even to be bored is to be changed. Sven Birkerts points out that the act of reading (especially fiction) posits an Elsewhere, another place beyond the present reality we inhabit. We read in order to travel, or be borne, to that other place and thus interrupt the curse of having only one life to lead.

Strange to say, but Marjorie Kinnan Rawlings' *The Yearling* (1938) finds itself in competition with Nabokov's *Lolita* (1955) for first prize in my life-changing category. As far as geographical tourism goes, *The Yearling*, which my mother first read to me, lifted me out of a childhood in New York City and set me down in the scrubland of north Florida, where a barefoot boy was free to roam an exotic terrain of palmetto, orange groves, and alligator swamps. *Lolita*, which I read secretly while ensconced in a Jesuit college, took me on a tour of an America I hadn't seen yet: a land of billboards, western scenery, and cheesy motels. And, of course, a tour of strange love.

What more deeply connects the two books—one written for children, the other about a seducer of children—is their capacity to expand the natural sympathies of the reader. A boy and his pet deer and a man and his nymphet seem an odd coupling, but they manage a similar effect. The plight of the deer and the fate of Lo arouse pity; but the doomed attempts to capture and control two essentially wild creatures elicit sympathy. No fence, however high, will contain the growing deer, and no amount of scheming and cajoling will keep the girl from growing into a woman. Her death in childbirth underscores, from Humbert's point of view, the fatal consequences of her maturation. If reading enlarges our sympathy for others, strangers mostly—here a boy and a man whose loves are doomed by their desire—then these two books, alien to each other, widened my world and awakened empathies I had never felt before.

BILLY COLLINS is the author of six books of poetry, including *The Trouble with Poetry and Other Poems*; *Picnic, Lightning*; *Sailing Alone Around the Room*; and *Questions About Angels*, which was selected by Edward Hirsch for the National Poetry Series. Collins' poetry has appeared in a variety of periodicals and in several volumes of *The Best American Poetry.* A New York Public Library Literary Lion, he is Distinguished Professor of English at Lehman College and editor of *Poetry 180*, an Internet project designed to make it easy for students to hear or read a poem on each of the 180 days of the school year. He has served as United States Poet Laureate (2001–2003) and is now New York State Poet Laureate (2004–2006).

The Nancy Drew Mysteries

Carolyn Keene

Claire Cook

Nancy Drew changed my life. Not once, not twice, but three times. That's a lot, even for Nancy.

When my mother died suddenly just before my eleventh birthday, I decided that spending time with Nancy was preferable to inhabiting my own life. So I disappeared into my mother's worn blue copy of *The Mystery at Lilac Inn* and quickly worked my way through the rest of her collection. I liked to close my eyes and pretend the pages smelled like my mother, though they actually smelled more like mildew. Even then I knew you could always imagine something better than reality. Nancy's world was fair and predictable. Though she'd lost her own mother, she seemed to be doing just fine. She even had a boyfriend. And a roadster.

I rediscovered Nancy when I was teaching writing to middle schoolers. I think you have to be an avid, joyful reader before you can be a writer, and some of the kids just weren't big readers yet. So we all lugged in a crazy assortment of things—novels, magazines, comic books, manga, biographies, encyclopedias. We swapped everything around and curled up in corners all over the room and just read. I brought Nancy, and a couple of the kids really took to her.

I remembered my own daughter's obsession with The Baby-Sitters Club, my son's addiction to Goosebumps. They just couldn't get enough of them. They picked up reading speed. They eventually moved on to other books and became lifelong readers. The truth, as I came to see it, is that once you fall in love, really in love, with that first book, you'll never be able to stop. There will still be plenty of time to introduce the classics. I give Nancy full credit for that teaching epiphany.

I revisited Nancy a third time just before I took a deep breath and finally dared to write my first novel. I was in my forties, sitting outside my daughter's swim practice at five in the morning. I was scared and Nancy was there for me. She taught me not to write the boring parts, the ones people skip over anyway. She taught me to keep my chapters short, and to end them in such a way that the reader just won't be able to put the book down.

Now, in my new life as a novelist, every once in a while I'll get a letter from a reader like this one.

> Dear Claire, all my life I've envied my friends who are readers. The truth is I am a slow reader and have never been able to enjoy it very much. I almost never finish the book. I am writing to tell you that someone gave me one of your books, and I couldn't put it down. I stayed up late two nights and FINISHED IT! After I read the rest of yours, I'm hoping you can suggest some other books I might enjoy.

Though our books are nothing alike, sometimes I think I might be channeling Nancy. Maybe I'll even get to drive her roadster someday.

CLAIRE COOK is the bestselling author of three novels, including *Must Love Dogs*, which has been adapted as a major motion picture starring Diane Lane and John Cusack, and *Multiple Choice*, which has been optioned for a movie by Working Title. She is hard at work on her fourth novel, *Take It or Leave It*, to be published by Hyperion in September 2007.

Caesar's Gallic Wars

JULIUS CAESAR

CAROLINE B. COONEY

I loved high school Latin, especially Julius Caesar's *Gallic Wars*, although at best I stumbled through, dependent on footnotes, and never did figure out what indirect discourse was. Our teacher transmitted her passion for this stately language and this brilliant commander. But for me, the thrill was to read in Caesar's own language the very dispatches he wrote some two thousand years before I was born.

Ever since, I have avidly read (in English) Roman history and ancient military history. Publication date doesn't matter to me: Napoleon III's 1838 analysis of the Gallic Wars, Tom Holland's 2003 *Rubicon*, Cicero's extant comments as he watched Caesar in action—I love them all. I love contemporary writers of ancient historical fiction—Colleen McCullough and Gillian Bradshaw, John Maddox Roberts and Steven Pressfield. But even though I had a substantial collection of books in Latin, I did not keep up my studies and gradually forgot everything except what you need for crossword puzzles.

When I turned fifty, I asked myself, What do I most want to do that I haven't yet done? I wanted to read Caesar again in Latin, and not be fourteen. I went back to school to relearn Latin, and ancient Greek was also offered. Why not? I thought. (It turns out there are thousands of reasons why not, mainly verbs, which are stupefyingly complex.) In second-semester Greek, however, I had that same shivery thrill—reading something that matters in its original language. Our class, spoon-fed by the professor, translated out loud the Gospel of John, and my turn included John 3:16: "For God so loved the world . . ." So after I reread the *Gallic Wars*, I read the Gospels in Greek, and in the Vulgate (the Latin Bible) I started with Genesis and I'm up to Judges.

I have two sorrows. My high school Latin teacher is no longer alive and I cannot tell her how much she changed and improved my life. And I don't know where I'm going to find the time (or the brains—it took me so long to make any progress in Greek) to take up Hebrew so I can do the Old Testament in its original language.

CAROLINE B. COONEY is the author of *The Face on the Milk Carton*, *Code Orange*, *Driver's Ed*, *Goddess of Yesterday*, and more than seventy other suspense novels for middle school readers, which together have sold more than fifteen million copies. She lives in Connecticut.

Uncle Tom's Cabin

Harriet Beecher Stowe

The Original Sin

Patricia Cornwell

I wish I had known Harriet Beecher Stowe, an alleged ancestor on my paternal grandmother's side of the family. I wish I could sit down with her now and talk about the crime that permeates our society, the slavery that may have changed its shape and form but not its fangs.

One of these days I'll get around to pursuing my precise ancestral connection to the Beechers, and I suspect it truly is there based on the family lore I have been hearing all my life, not necessarily positive tales, as my grandmother, G.G., who would have been six when Harriet died, had nothing but contempt for her and the Beecher family. Most of G.G.'s animosity sprang from her anti-evangelical Christian sensibilities, and in a way I find that an irony today, when so much of what is rabidly right wing I associate with exactly what Harriet was passionately against.

Abuse of power. Deciding a group of people does not deserve the same rights as others. Discrimination. Violation of privacy, of civil liberties. Supremacism based on race, religion, gender, politics, sexual orientation. I could go on. Philosophically, all of it is there in *Uncle Tom's Cabin*, which influenced a nation and caused Harriet to be deeply hated by the South because most Southerners never quite understood that her novel wasn't a condemnation of them as individuals but of the institution of slavery. Typically, people don't easily budge from their opinions of what an author is saying (usually because they haven't read the book and never will).

Times change? Well. . . . About a hundred and forty years after *Uncle Tom's Cabin* was published, I happened to host a book signing for Joan Hedrick and her Pulitzer Prize–winning biography of Harriet Beecher Stowe, the setting, Richmond, Virginia, where Harriet remains unwelcome and probably most of the people in that former capital of the Confederacy still haven't read her famed if not infamous work. No members of the media appeared, and scarcely anybody would have shown up at the small but gutsy independent bookstore had I not prevailed upon my friends. Afterward, a few well-meaning acquaintances in my Richmond neighborhood suggested to me that if I wanted to host a book signing for another author, Shelby Foote would be a better idea.

I don't remember the first time I read *Uncle Tom's Cabin,* but I am forever mindful of its impact on me. It isn't so much Harriet's prose or her vivid characterizations or her painful depictions of cruelty that have touched me and shaded my own writing, but our shared belief that all unfairness, harshness, and inevitable violence are born of the same original sin: the abuse of power, the ultimate result of which is enslavement, impoverishment, suffering, and death.

PATRICIA CORNWELL's recent bestsellers include *Predator, Trace*, and *Portrait of a Killer: Jack the Ripper—Case Closed*. Her newest thriller, *At Risk*, originally appeared in *The New York Times Magazine*'s Sunday Serial and was published by Putnam in May 2006. Patricia Cornwell is director of Applied Forensic Science at the National Forensic Academy. Visit her Web site at www.patriciacornwell.com.

David Copperfield

Charles Dickens

Maureen Corrigan

I opened it up at the ideal moment in life, if not in the most ideal surroundings. I was thirteen and riding on the Q60 bus that goes up and down Queens Boulevard from the farthest reaches of Forest Hills to its soaring final run up and over the Fifty-ninth Street Bridge and into its last stop on Second Avenue in Manhattan. I was antsy that Saturday and wanted to escape my parents and our small apartment in Sunnyside, Queens. None of my girlfriends were around, so I rode off by myself to the Macy's in Rego Park—a more exotic destination than the Robert Halls in the neighborhood. I wandered listlessly for a few hours around the department store aisles and tried on poor boy sweaters and shift dresses with Empire waistlines. At thirteen, I wanted to look like Susan Dey from *The Partridge Family*, with her goofy smile and blue eyes and shiny straight brown hair and perfect skin. At thirteen, I too had brown hair and blue eyes, but my complexion was a torment, my own personal cross to bear, as the nuns in my Catholic grammar school would have said. The twice-monthly dermatologist visits that my sympathetic mother paid for only made things worse. The "skin doctor" tried to bake away my acne with a sun lamp, the result being that I sported pimples *and* red flaking skin throughout the week. "You've got dandruff of the face!" joked another dermatologist in the office. To be a thirteen-year-old girl with acne and dandruff of the face . . . no wonder I walked around all the time with my nose stuck in a book.

What a relief, then, on the ride home, to escape my face (seen in too many dressing room mirrors that afternoon) and my unlovely Queens surroundings by opening up a paperback of *David Copperfield*, the book the "English nun" had assigned my class that week. In the first sentence, I found my soul mate. "Whether I shall turn out to be the hero of my own life, or whether that station will be held by anybody else, these pages must show." David Copperfield, in his opening address to the reader, voiced my own adolescent sense of grandiosity and anxiety: I yearned for distinction, yet I sensed I was destined to be swallowed up in mediocrity, never to rise above the crowd like Susan Dey.

As I raced through the early chapters, I loved how Dickens dramatized the life of a boy so completely at the mercy of adults, some flawed (like his flighty, doomed mother and the kindly but ignorant Peggotty), some downright vile (like his bewhiskered ogre of a stepfather, Mr. Murdstone). And after the death of his mother, when David is cast off into that infernal "blacking factory," the terror of his situation—the terror of being ground down over years and years by stupid, exhausting work—so overwhelmed me that I couldn't sleep that night, until my worried parents allowed me to stay up and read my way into David's deliverance. For many, many years afterward, throughout all the after-school and summer jobs I worked in factory offices, five-and-tens, and stockrooms, I would flash on David toiling away at Murdstone and Grinby's. I saw those jobs as so many incarnations of the blacking factory, not because they were cruel or soul-destroying, but because they were mindless and—like David, and like Dickens himself—I thought that there were few things worse than to be buried alive in a lifetime of mindless work. Too many people in my family had been swallowed up by those kinds of jobs. Reading *David Copperfield* that first time at age thirteen fired my resolve to find work that would be satisfying in some way and draw upon whatever gifts I had. I knew I was good at writing—I'd won the school song contest by writing an anthem to my parochial school, St. Raphael's, to the tune of Petula Clark's "Downtown." Maybe, like Dickens, I too could write myself out of whatever blacking factories loomed ahead.

Thirteen is an age of extremes. I wasn't really threatened by a future of grinding labor, because my working-class parents had started a college fund for me when I was born. And though I didn't know it then, I wasn't going to be another Dickens either. But I did eventually find writing work I love, work that has given me a sense of purpose and distinction. I reread *David Copperfield* every few years, and while I feel more insulated from its terrors as an adult, I never fail to be touched by them. The wonder of how Dickens creates a world that breathes out of such explicit artifice—madmen flying kites, jolly families at home in debtor's prison, oily monsters lurking in the shadows—has never left me. If I couldn't write a *David Copperfield*, I'm thrilled to have found a career that lets me admire it in print, along with all the other amazing works of literature, contemporary and classic, that crowd our library and bookstore shelves.

MAUREEN CORRIGAN is the book critic for the NPR program *Fresh Air*, and the author of the recent literary memoir *Leave Me Alone, I'm Reading.*

Atlas Shrugged

AYN RAND

and more

NELSON DEMILLE

There have actually been four books that changed my life: George Orwell's *1984* and *Animal Farm*, Aldous Huxley's *Brave New World*, and Ayn Rand's *Atlas Shrugged*. Note that these are all dystopian novels, which would be interesting to a mental health provider.

I read these novels in college between 1962 and 1966, and I must admit I chose the first three because they were short. The fourth, Rand's *Atlas Shrugged,* like most of her novels, is anything but short, and this was the one that had the most profound influence on me. Rand is nowhere near the writer that Orwell or Huxley was, but in many ways she's a deeper thinker, and ultimately, as the decades pass, she may have had the best crystal ball.

Books people read and discuss during the formative years of their lives usually have the greatest effect on their thinking. Obviously, young people are impressionable, and the world of ideas is new to eighteen-year-olds entering college—especially if, like most American kids, they didn't learn much in high school.

For me, a college student of the post-1950s, pre-Vietnam era, the philosophy put forth in *Atlas Shrugged*—which Rand called Objectivism—seemed like a romantic underground movement, esoteric and elite, with its own jargon, superheroes, and very unconventional (for the time) ideas about morality, religion, government, and society.

Ironically, though Rand and her philosophy are often considered to be of the political right, many of her beliefs, and the beliefs of the characters in her novels, were precursors to what we would soon be calling the counterculture of the left.

The thing about *Atlas Shrugged* that so impressed me then, and still impresses me, is that Rand's ideas can't be categorized or pigeonholed as liberal or conservative. Though Rand can be dogmatic and polemic, she was an original thinker who gave us a third option for how to live our lives, as well as an alternate view of how the world works.

I never completely bought into Objectivism, but it certainly upset my well-ordered post-Eisenhower world, and jarred me into what we'd today call thinking outside the box.

NELSON DEMILLE is the bestselling author of twelve novels, among them *By the Rivers of Babylon*, *Cathedral*, *The General's Daughter*, *Plum Island*, *The Lion's Game*, *Up Country*, *Night Fall*, and most recently *Wild Fire.* Born in New York City and raised on Long Island, he attended Hofstra University for three years and then joined the army. He was commissioned as a first lieutenant, saw action in Vietnam as an infantry platoon leader with the First Cavalry Division, and was decorated with the Air Medal, the Bronze Star, and the Vietnamese Cross of Gallantry. After completing his service, he returned to Hofstra and earned a degree in political science and history. He has two children, Lauren and Alexander, and still lives on Long Island.

Kristin Lavransdatter

Sigrid Undset

Tomie dePaola

I am a fickle reader. Nothing brings that fact home to me more clearly than when I am asked, "What book made you a lifelong reader?" or "What one book would you encourage people to read?" Or, even better, "What book changed your life?" or that wonderful party game, "If you were stranded on a desert island and you could have only one book with you, what would it be?" My answers—yes, answers—have ranged from the Bible to the *I Ching* or even to the book I was right in the middle of and was not willing to let go of. So, I am fickle.

I've told my young readers that *Hitty: Her First Hundred Years*, by Rachel Field (the original edition), was my favorite book as a child. But then, I've also said that the Greek legends as retold by Nathaniel Hawthorne stole my heart and imagination. Then there was *Homer Price,* by Robert McCloskey. I suspect that had more to do with Kresge's five-and-dime getting a post–World War II doughnut machine installed right around the same time that the doughnut machine played such an important part in Homer's life.

But I am mature in years now. Time to put fickleness aside and make a wise choice of an important book in my life. I could say the Bible or the *I Ching.* I could say *Hitty* or *Homer.* I won't say *Charlotte's Web* or *The Lord of the Rings.*

But as hard as I try, a trilogy keeps creeping into my heart. I read it for the first time in 1957, on a snowy day, afternoon, and evening into morning, in a very primitive Vermont farmhouse where I was living with a friend, Jack Schanhaar. Jack had given me a Modern Library copy of this remarkable book (or books), and when I started to read, I couldn't stop. I read right through the night, stopping only when I had finished. In a sort of ritualistic way, I reread this book every winter until 1962, when I left Vermont for another kind of life. I still reread it, again and again, although not annually. I always find something new in it.

The book is the trilogy *Kristin Lavransdatter*, by Sigrid Undset.

Now that I have revealed my first mature love, I realize that I am still fickle. If you haven't read this next trilogy, you must: Philip Pullman's His Dark Materials (*The Golden Compass*, *The Subtle Knife*, and *The Amber Spyglass*). It is the love of my old age. I am in the midst of rereading it again this winter in a pretty classy house in New Hampshire.

But then, how about the Bible, the *I Ching*, *Hitty* . . .

I wonder what's next.

TOMIE DEPAOLA is best known for the more than two hundred books he has written and/or illustrated for children. His newest book is *Christmas Remembered*, a book for all ages. He has received the Caldecott Honor, the Newbery Honor, and the Lotte Jacobi Living Treasure Award of the New Hampshire Governor's Arts Awards. You can learn more at www.tomie.com.

A Room of One's Own

VIRGINIA WOOLF

ANITA DIAMANT

A Room of One's Own influenced me as a journalist and as a novelist in ways that continue to unfold. I'm pretty sure that I missed the humor on virtually every page when I first read the essay, as an earnest undergraduate, but the underlinings and exclamation points in my college paperback ($1.95!) remind me of the impact it had on me then. Today when I reread it, I'm still inspired, not only by Woolf's clear-eyed message that women's stories need to be told, but also by her style, conviction, and wit. Written in 1928, these 118 pages still challenge readers and writers to consider who is left out.

In one memorable passage, Woolf ponders the lives of the flesh-and-blood women who were Shakespeare's contemporaries.

> One knows nothing detailed, nothing perfectly true and substantial about [the Elizabethan woman]. History scarcely mentions her. . . . She never writes her own life and scarcely keeps a diary; there are only a handful of her letters in existence. She left no plays or poems by which we can judge her. What one wants . . . is a mass of information; at what age did she marry; how many children had she as a rule; what was her house like; had she a room to herself; did she do the cooking. . . . All these facts lie somewhere, presumably, in parish registers and account books; the life of the average Elizabethan woman must be scattered about somewhere, could one collect it and make a book of it.

Virginia Woolf challenged me to write *The Red Tent.* And *Good Harbor.* And *The Last Days of Dogtown*—and probably everything else I'll scribble for the rest of my life. Thanks to *A Room of One's Own*, I want to tell stories that have fallen (or might yet) off the page of history simply because they belong to women.

In the case of *The Red Tent*, a historical novel set in biblical times, there were no letters or parish records to consult. The historical record has almost nothing to say about the ordinary lives of women before the nineteenth century, and even when it does, working women, poor women, and women of color remain invisible, forgotten, and often nameless. "One often catches a glimpse of them in the lives of the great, whisking away into the background," writes Virginia Woolf, "concealing, I sometimes think, a wink, a laugh, perhaps a tear."

In Genesis 34, there is a glimpse of Dinah, daughter of Leah and Jacob, heading off to visit the daughters of Shechem. We have no diary, no letters, no testimony from Dinah about what happened to her in that ancient city. The tale of Jacob and his sons includes a brutal footnote about that adventure, but it is not told in Dinah's voice. It is not her version.

What did Dinah do in Shechem? What was she wearing? What did she see and feel and learn? *The Red Tent* is my answer. But the question was first put to me by Virginia Woolf in *A Room of One's Own*.

ANITA DIAMANT's first novel, *The Red Tent*, became a word-of-mouth bestseller, won the 2001 Book Sense Book of the Year Award, and has been published in twenty-five countries. She is the author of two other novels, *Good Harbor* and *The Last Days of Dogtown*; a collection of essays, *Pitching My Tent: On Marriage, Motherhood, Friendship, and Other Leaps of Faith*; and six nonfiction guides to contemporary Jewish life, including *How to Be a Jewish Parent* and *Saying Kaddish*. An award-winning journalist, she has written for *The Boston Globe Magazine*, *Parenting*, *Yankee*, and *Reform Judaism*, among other publications. She lives in the Boston area and is founder and president of Mayyim Hayyim: Living Waters Community Mikveh and Education Center (www.mayyimhayyim.org).

The Way We Live Now

ANTHONY TROLLOPE

DOMINICK DUNNE

For more than half my life, it has been my curious lot to move among the rich and famous and powerful, always as an outsider, always listening, watching, remembering. Although I didn't start writing until I was fifty years old, an observer's eye had been observing for forty of those fifty years.

In 1973, my career as a producer and studio executive in television and movies had come to a permanent halt. I left Hollywood like a whipped dog and drove to the Cascade Mountains of Oregon—where I had never been, where I knew no one, but the name Cascade Mountains evoked a kind of peace in me that I desperately needed.

The thought of writing had been lurking within me for some time, but I kept pushing it away, fearful that I was inadequate for such a task as writing a book, and fearful also that it might be a further act of failure. In a hamlet called Camp Sherman I rented a one-room cabin that happened to have neither a telephone nor a television set. I remained there for six months. I lived in virtual silence. I walked in the forest. I fed the birds. I licked the wounds of failure in both marriage and career. I'd brought along a bag of books that I had been meaning to read during the years when my reading was dominated by scripts and outlines. I had forgotten the sheer joy of reading a great novel, the total immersion of self into other people's lives.

In that tiny cabin, sitting on an orange Naugahyde chair

with a broken spring in the seat, I read the book that changed my life, although I was unaware of it at the time. Then I only knew that I was transfixed by *The Way We Live Now*, a novel about London society, written by Anthony Trollope in 1875. I didn't want it to end. It showed a panorama of class, wealth, power, snobbery, social climbing, advantageous marrying, gambling away family fortunes, all set in a world of dinner parties, balls, and men's clubs, where the divine and the despicable mix. The inner workings of society have always fascinated me. In Augustus Melmotte, the richest man in London, an outsider of mysterious background, for whom there never can be enough money, Trollope created one of the great characters in fiction. A swindling financier, Melmotte resembles the billionaires we read about today as they are being indicted or hauled off to prison for some sort of financial malfeasance, like stealing from their stockholders.

After my Oregon experience, I moved to New York and became a writer. Eight years later, after I had published several novels, I reread *The Way We Live Now* for the third time. The parallels between the London society of the 1870s and the New York society of the 1980s were astonishing. I decided to write my own version of Trollope's book, about what I was witnessing on a nightly basis in the drawing rooms of New York as the possessors of the new vast fortunes overtook the Old Guard of the city. My book was called *People Like Us.* My Augustus Melmotte character was Elias Renthal, who goes to prison for his misdeeds after his dazzling social climb to the top ranks of financial and philanthropic New York. The book was a popular success, and a glamorous television miniseries followed. It infuriated many of the people, and rightly so, who identified themselves in my characters.

Anthony Trollope, whose literary output was enormous, became my favorite writer. I have read almost all of his forty-seven novels. I have learned so much from him. He understood that even villains have their charming moments. He understood the world of the rich and powerful as well as the duc de Saint-Simon did in his diaries of the court of Louis XIV, or Marcel Proust did in his brilliant *Remembrance of Things Past.* I will always treasure my six months in the cabin in the Cascade Mountains of Oregon, where I first read the book that has so influenced my writing.

DOMINICK DUNNE has been a contributing editor to *Vanity Fair* since 1984 and is now a special correspondent. He has covered such high-profile, million-dollar defense trials as those of O. J. Simpson, William Kennedy Smith, Erik and Lyle Menendez, and Robert Blake. He has also written revealing pieces on some of the world's most fascinating people, including Imelda Marcos, Robert Mapplethorpe, Elizabeth Taylor, and Queen Noor of Jordan. Dunne's bestselling novels, almost all of which have been made into television miniseries, include *The Two Mrs. Grenvilles*, *An Inconvenient Woman*, *People Like Us*, *A Season in Purgatory*, and *Another City, Not My Own.* He has also published three collections of essays, *The Mansions of Limbo*, *Fatal Charms*, and *Justice*, as well as a photo memoir, *The Way We Lived Then.* He is currently at work on another novel, *A Solo Act.*

The Imitation of Christ

THOMAS À KEMPIS

CARLOS EIRE

Books have made me who I am. No doubt about it. I think this holds true for every reader, to some degree. Little by little we change and grow as we read. Even rotten books can sometimes make us wiser. And then there are books that change us substantially and put us on a new path. Every reader has a list of such books. In my case, when I was eight, Mark Twain's *Tom Sawyer* got me hooked on reading. In my first year of graduate school, Roland Bainton's biography of Martin Luther, *Here I Stand*, convinced me to specialize in Reformation history rather than in medieval theology. In my last year of graduate school, Dashiell Hammett's *The Thin Man* and Raymond Chandler's *The Big Sleep* taught me how to write. When I was about to turn thirty, reading two books in my native tongue—Guillermo Cabrera Infante's *Tres tristes tigres* (*Three Trapped Tigers*) and Gabriel García Márquez's *Cien años de soledad* (*One Hundred Years of Solitude*)—allowed me to reclaim my Spanish identity.

But there is only one book that truly changed my life, inside and out, and from top to bottom: Thomas à Kempis's *The Imitation of Christ.* When I arrived in the United States in 1962, at the age of eleven, without my parents, and without a clue as to where I would end up, the only thing I had in my pocket was this fifteenth-century devotional manual. The Cuban authorities would not let us bring along any money, jewelry, or photographs, or more than two changes of clothing, but graciously allowed us the luxury of fleeing with one book. A single book, that was it. The smaller the better, for there were also very strict size and weight limits imposed on our luggage. Much to my chagrin, *The Imitation of Christ* happened to be the one text my family had chosen for me.

As I bounced around from foster home to foster home in the United States, I grew attached to the book, not because I liked to read it—hell, no—but simply because it was one of the very few mementos that linked me physically with my family. It might as well have been a rabbit foot or some other useless trinket, for although I handled it often and kept it close to me, I never read it. Every now and then I would open it at random, take a look at a sentence or two, and shut it immediately. Not only did it seem useless and dull: it scared me half to death. It spoke of suffering and redemption, of emptying oneself, and of dying in order to be reborn. Every page reminded me of crucifixes and crowns of thorns and nails driven through hands and feet. It scared me more than any horror film or any dark, empty church or any graveyard. Still, I felt compelled to look into it regularly, for it brought me closer to those who had given it to me, whom I missed terribly.

Very, very slowly, the book began to speak to me. As months of separation from my loved ones turned to years, and as I matured, what had once frightened me out of my wits began to seem sweet, even inebriating. Gradually, I began to read the book and embrace what it had to say, which boiled down to this: pain can be redeeming. *The Imitation of Christ* introduced me to the art of introspection and taught me to look for God in the smallest details. It also let me know that in a world where suffering, death, and moral failure are inevitable, the only real treasures are intangible, and that the greatest three things on earth are faith, hope, and love.

CARLOS EIRE is the Riggs Professor of History and Religious Studies at Yale University. Before joining the Yale faculty in 1996, he taught at St. John's University and the University of Virginia, and resided for two years at the Institute for Advanced Study in Princeton. He is the author of several books on sixteenth- and seventeenth-century European history, but is more widely known for his memoir of the Cuban Revolution, *Waiting for Snow in Havana*, which won the National Book Award for Nonfiction in 2003.

The Adventures of Sherlock Holmes

ARTHUR CONAN DOYLE

LINDA FAIRSTEIN

Perhaps part of the thrill of discovering the book that changed my life was that it was purloined. I can't remember a time when reading, or being read to, was not among my greatest pleasures. My older brother had other interests, so when I saw him carrying a thick book around everywhere for several weeks, I was determined to find out what had engaged him so. I was eleven when I spirited his dog-eared volume of *The Adventures of Sherlock Holmes* out of his room under the cover of darkness and began to read the reminiscences of Dr. John Watson.

I started with "A Study in Scarlet"—Conan Doyle's first published story—and raced through the entire collection in a matter of days. But it is "The Adventure of the Speckled Band" that stands out as my strongest memory of my early infatuation with the great Holmes. To this day I can call up images of the terrified young woman who presents herself in the detective's sitting room, a return train ticket in her hand and her mud-spattered jacket drawing Holmes' attention; of her stepfather, back from Calcutta, with a changed disposition and a passion for Indian animals; and of the tragic death of her twin sister under most mysterious circumstances. Nothing prepared me for the solution of the case, terrified of snakes as I am, and I have been grateful ever after that I had neither a ventilator nor a bellpull in my bedroom.

I loved everything about the tales—the brilliance and elegance of Sherlock Holmes, the use of his powers of careful observation and deduction to recognize the clues that would solve the crime, the formality yet intimacy of the storyteller's language, and the powerful sense of place, whether London or Peshawar or an ancestral home in the English countryside.

Holmes was my first introduction to a mature, well-educated, skillful crime solver. The stories I'd been crafting for my school newspaper at the time, my first steps toward becoming a writer, featured adolescent imitations of Nancy Drew. Reading Conan Doyle's stories spurred my ambition to hold an intelligent audience spellbound with well-told tales, meticulous plotting, and a clever denouement for every situation. I have picked up Holmes' adventures over and over again throughout the years, never failing to be caught up in the world Conan Doyle so brilliantly depicts. I can't think of any gift greater than being able to entertain so many generations of readers all around the world.

My very loving father was also quite practical, especially whenever I announced that I planned to be a writer. Even in my college years, when I was majoring in English literature, he used to advise me that I had nothing to write about so I'd better get myself a job. I spent thirty years as a prosecutor in the Manhattan District Attorney's Office, handling homicides and other violent felonies, and I can't help but think that my first detecting hero, Sherlock Holmes, was as responsible as my father for inspiring that part of my career. Holmes is, after all, the only fictional character ever made an honorary fellow of the Royal Society of Chemistry because of his contributions to forensic investigation.

LINDA FAIRSTEIN is the bestselling author of *Final Jeopardy*, *Likely to Die*, *Cold Hit*, and five other Alexandra Cooper crime novels, most recently *Death Dance*. A fellow of the American

College of Trial Lawyers and a member of the International Society of Barristers, she headed the Sex Crimes Unit of the Manhattan District Attorney's Office for twenty-five years, and recounted her experiences there in *Sexual Violence*, a New York Times Notable Book of 1994. She and her husband divide their time between Manhattan and Martha's Vineyard.

The Guns of August

BARBARA W. TUCHMAN

DORIS KEARNS GOODWIN

I was a sophomore in college when I read Barbara Tuchman's *The Guns of August*—a book so stunning that I have read it a dozen times since then. Though I had loved reading history ever since I was a child, this enthralling work inspired me to think that I might someday write history of my own. Tuchman published her book in 1962, before women's liberation had truly taken hold. Yet here was a woman who had not only entered the field of war writing traditionally reserved to men but had carried away all the honors in so doing.

The beauty of the first sentence still amazes me. "So gorgeous was the spectacle on the May morning of 1910 when nine kings rode in the funeral of Edward VII of England that the crowd, waiting in hushed and black-clad awe, could not keep back gasps of admiration." And the quality of Tuchman's prose never falters from that spectacular start to the very end. I remember thinking then that I would give almost anything I had to be able to write like that.

I read the book over a long weekend. I could not put it down. I had to find out what was going to happen next. Here was a master storyteller who understood, as she later wrote in *Practicing History*, that you had to tell a story as it naturally unfolds, "without using the benefit of hindsight, resisting always the temptation to refer to events still ahead," so that the reader is kept in suspense at every step along the way, even to the point of not knowing how the war is going to end.

I'd like to think that I learned from her, not only how to tell a story, but how to make the characters come alive. For I believe, as Barbara Tuchman did, that narrative is "the lifeblood of history," and that the best way to tell the tale is to immerse oneself in primary sources—diaries, letters, pamphlets, memoirs, newspapers, oral histories. Such materials are gold to the historian, for they provide the telling details—the look of a face, the sound of a voice, the reaction to a loss—that allow the reader to feel as if he or she is truly present at the scene.

Perhaps the greatest lesson Barbara Tuchman taught, however, was the importance of "being in love with your subject." Her passion for the dramatic events of World War I shines through on every page. I have followed her advice, making sure when I choose my subjects that I look forward to waking up with them every morning and going to bed with them every night! For this, and for teaching me the craft of history, I shall always be grateful to Barbara Tuchman. She is my heroine.

DORIS KEARNS GOODWIN is the bestselling author of *Lyndon Johnson and the American Dream*; *The Fitzgeralds and the Kennedys*; *Wait Till Next Year*, a memoir of growing up in the 1950s in love with the Brooklyn Dodgers; and most recently *Team of Rivals: The Political Genius of Abraham Lincoln*, which was awarded the 2006 Lincoln Prize. *No Ordinary Time*, her chronicle of the Roosevelts and the home front during World War II, won the 1995 Pulitzer Prize in History. She is an analyst for NBC News, a member of the Society of American Historians and the American Academy of Arts and Sciences, and the recipient of the Sara Josepha Hale Medal and the Charles Frankel Prize of the National Endowment for the Humanities.

The Perfect Storm

SEBASTIAN JUNGER

LINDA GREENLAW

One day this past holiday season I was thrilled to find a mysterious package at the post office. I rushed home and ripped open the sizable box. Cookies! The gorgeous tin of assorted goodies joined me on the couch, where I sat to read the accompanying card, containing an invitation to write an essay on "the book that changed my life." I nibbled a rich, buttery confection and contemplated this request for my thoughts. Imagining other authors writing of profound changes in the wake of Homer's *Odyssey* (a book that made me regret having learned to read), I wondered if I should expose the depth of my shallowness. My initial thought was to write about *The Perricone Weight-Loss Diet.* This book has had quite a staggering effect on my consumption. Although I have not lost an ounce (thanks in part to the cookies), I am eating sardines every day and taking fish oil pills. My skin looks great.

My next bright idea was to write about how my life has been shaped by books that I have *not* read. Imagine how much smarter I would be if I had read everything assigned and recommended! If I had studied more in school and read more literature, perhaps I would never have gone fishing. In many respects, my life has been most significantly affected by what I have neglected to read. Take, for instance, the advance reading copy of the book in need of a blurb that sits awaiting my enthusiastic endorsement. Not reading this book has definitely changed my life. I find myself checking the caller ID before answering the phone so as to avoid the author, and am suffering twinges of guilt. But this does not answer the question.

It's obvious! *The Perfect Storm* changed my life. I survived the Halloween Gale of 1991. Other fishermen were not so lucky. Along came an extraordinary journalist named Sebastian Junger. Then, along came his book. And before I knew it, I was known by people other than my family, fellow fishermen, and the bartender at the Crow's Nest. This was entirely the result of other people's reading of *The Perfect Storm*. Of course I read the book too—the whole book, not just the parts that mentioned me, which I couldn't have found otherwise because there's no index.

And what happened was this. The reading of that book changed my life in two ways. It literally changed my life by bringing with it the opportunity to write my own books. But it also changed my life because it reminded me of something I knew, that the lives of the people around me—captains, owners, fishermen—were lives that had real dignity and drama and deserved to be chronicled. That these men and women, all flawed, some crazy, some sober, many drunk, a few sane, were every bit as worthy of being written about as any other type of people who appear in books. I'm not discounting Sebastian's considerable skill in bringing these people, including me, to life. But the very fact that he chose us made me think about myself and others in a different way, not just as people but as characters.

Other writers have helped give me my voice—I think I've taken inspiration from everyone from Sarah Orne Jewett to Pat Conroy. But what *The Perfect Storm* gave me was an awareness of my subject. And like most things you go questing for, it turned out to be right under my very nose.

LINDA GREENLAW is the bestselling author of *All Fishermen Are Liars, The Lobster Chronicles,* and *The Hungry Ocean,* and is coauthor with her mother, Martha Greenlaw, of the cookbook *Recipes from a Very Small Island*. She lives on Isle au Haut, Maine.

The Reason Why

CECIL WOODHAM-SMITH

DAVID HALBERSTAM

When I was a junior in college in 1954, a friend gave me a copy of Cecil Woodham-Smith's *The Reason Why*, which had just been published in America. It's the story of why the Light Brigade marched into the Valley of Death during the Crimean War. I was absolutely in awe of Woodham-Smith's accomplishment. She had taken a story that was factual (like any schoolboy, I knew the rough outline from the Tennyson poem, but that was about all I knew) and turned it into a breathtaking tale that read like a novel.

The Reason Why is not so much about heroism and the validation of courage as it is a tale of foolishness, of a class system that produced monsters as commanders, men who were allowed to buy their commissions. It was my introduction to what you might call the glitches of history, that is, all the things they don't tell you in high school history classes. What struck me at the time was how simply but beautifully written it was, so different from all the history books I had been forced to read thus far in my life. Here was history that was fun and accessible. I knew from the moment I started it that I was in the hands of a master, that she could evoke a time and era brilliantly. For at its heart *The Reason Why* is a portrait of a class system destroying an army, and the commanders, Lords Raglan and Cardigan and Lucan, are not merely fools and incompetents but the embodiment of an era. I think that was when I began to consider trying to write nonfiction books myself, little knowing that fewer than twenty years later I would be a reporter in Vietnam and find all too many of the same glitches and write a book about the catastrophic road to that war.

A few weeks ago I went on vacation, and at the last minute I went over to a local library and checked out *The Reason Why.* I read it again and was thrilled to find that it was as rich a literary journey as ever and still had a wonderful hold over me. After I finished, I passed it on to the friends who were with us, and *The Reason Why* was informally voted the best book that anyone in our group had brought along on the trip

One of America's most distinguished journalists and historians, DAVID HALBERSTAM graduated from Harvard in 1955 and covered the early civil rights movement for the Nashville *Tennessean.* In 1964 his dispatches from Vietnam won him the Pulitzer Prize for International Reporting. He was the author of many bestselling works of nonfiction, including *The Best and the Brightest, The Powers That Be, Freedom Riders, War in a Time of Peace,* and such classic sports books as *The Breaks of the Game, Summer of '49, October 1964, Playing for Keeps,* and *The Education of a Coach.*

The Catcher in the Rye

J. D. Salinger

Alice Hoffman

I found *The Catcher in the Rye* on my mother's bookshelf. It was the cover that drew me to it. I was in eighth grade, I knew nothing, and I had certainly never heard of J. D. Salinger. So it was the cover—that somber unadorned maroon paperback, the literary equivalent of a brown paper bag—that made me feel as though I'd stumbled onto a secret. Whatever was inside was powerful, that much was certain. One hundred proof.

Published in 1951, the year before I was born, *The Catcher in the Rye* felt so oddly intimate, so very here and now, that sitting out in my backyard, reading underneath the willow tree, I felt as though the novel had been written expressly for me. The stream of consciousness, the intensity of Holden Caulfield's vision of the world as a haunted and haunting place, the cynicism, the truth, the sorrow, all of it blew me away. I had never had this kind of literary experience before—the gut-wrenching interactiveness of fiction. The sense that while reading someone else's creation, you, as a reader and as a person, are miraculously known and revealed.

The Catcher in the Rye is a coming-of-age story, perhaps the best ever written, but it is so much more. It is the revelation of the power of a single voice. The plot itself, the journey of one teenage boy, is less important than the emotion and the unique humanity. Reading a book became an act of intimacy. Take in a breath and don't let it out until you get to the last page.

In my own writing that is also the place I aim for—the inner heart of the story, the voice that sounds like no one else's yet feels personal and intimate. Fiction that doesn't just tell a story but tells readers something about what is deep within themselves. The "inside outness" of *The Catcher in the Rye*, the sense that as one reads the facts of the story there is an inner core that is being revealed at the very same time, is what I yearn for as both a reader and a writer.

The subject matter of *The Catcher in the Rye*—one teenager's angst-filled journey—convinced me that it is the telling that matters. I want to know everything about you, I remember thinking about Holden, as if he were real, more real than the people walking down my street. Clearly, Holden already knew me, far better than any of my friends. I felt the same way he did; I was as much an outsider, as haunted by deeds done and undone. That was the true discovery when I found that maroon book on the shelf in our living room—the power of fiction.

ALICE HOFFMAN is the author of fifteen acclaimed novels, including *The Ice Queen*, *Practical Magic*, and *Here on Earth*, as well as the highly praised story collections *Blackbird House* and *Local Girls*.

Bury My Heart at Wounded Knee

DEE BROWN

SEBASTIAN JUNGER

When I was about fifteen, I read *Bury My Heart at Wounded Knee*, by Dee Brown. It is a beautifully written book about the rapid and brutal conquest of North America by the fledgling American nation. I had read about that conquest—usually referred to as the "Indian Wars"—in various history classes in grade school and high school, but Dee Brown seemed to tell a very different story. It wasn't a story about victory; it was essentially a story about war crimes. I didn't know the term *war crimes* at the time, but I was old enough to know right from wrong. And what I was reading in those pages definitely seemed wrong.

As a journalist who has covered many poor, war-torn countries, I have come to two determinations. First of all, the United States, where I live, is one of the most free, open, and egalitarian countries in the world. The second is that every country has something dark and shameful in its past, and it will never be free to criticize other countries until that history is confronted. French objections to the U.S. invasion of Iraq are moot until France acknowledges the atrocities and war crimes its government committed in Algeria in the 1950s. Likewise, for the United States, our noble championing of liberty and democracy in the Middle East rings hollow until we acknowledge our efforts to undermine those very things in Central America in the 1980s, and in many other parts of the world.

The ethnic cleansing of North America is our original sin,

and out of it we have created a great and relatively just nation. But we will not fully merit the designation *democracy* until we have faced that ugly era of our nation's history. We wiped out 90 percent of the native population—even using Gatling guns against Sioux and Cheyenne villages in the last years of the conflict. By any modern standard, that is genocide. Dee Brown's great service was to bring that painful truth to a country he clearly loved.

SEBASTIAN JUNGER's latest book, *A Death in Belmont*, was published in April 2006 by W. W. Norton. He is also the author of *Fire* and the international bestseller *The Perfect Storm*. A contributing editor for *Vanity Fair*, he is the recipient of a National Magazine Award and an SAIS-Novartis Prize for Excellence in International Journalism. He lives in New York City and on Cape Cod.

An Introduction to Contemporary History

GEOFFREY BARRACLOUGH

PAUL KENNEDY

For many years, even in my time in high school, I had been fascinated by international affairs, and especially by military and diplomatic history. I was one of those precocious English schoolboys who, by the age of sixteen, knew everything there was to know about B-17 bombers and Spitfire fighters. Distinguishing a frigate from a destroyer was as easy as anything. As I went on to college (the University of Newcastle) and then to graduate school (St. Antony's, Oxford), my focus shifted, but only slightly, to diplomatic and colonial history, the scramble for Africa, and all that. My Oxford doctoral dissertation was on Great Power rivalries for relatively obscure islands in the South Pacific. These were my fields of interest, traditional stuff, fascinating (to me), and with very distinct boundaries.

But as a young university teacher I encountered a book that changed my life, or at least massively added to it. The title was *An Introduction to Contemporary History* (1964), and the author was Geoffrey Barraclough, a distinguished medieval historian who had recently undergone a conversion to the study of contemporary history—and very contemporary history at that. In this book, which was composed as a series of lectures given at Oxford and UCLA in the early 1960s, Barraclough posed a very simple question: what were the chief changes that had occurred in the world since the fall of Bismarck, back in spring 1890?

Forget this or that diplomatic treaty, or this or that naval action. What were the big historical movements of modern times?

Barraclough had his own answers: the impact of science and technology; the dwarfing of Europe; the coming of mass democracy; the population explosion; the revolt against the West. No doubt every reader can produce his or her own short list, and some will differ. That doesn't matter. The fact is that Barraclough had asked the big question. In an age of ever narrower specialists, he had rescued what might be called "large History," of the sort one associates with H. G. Wells or Gibbon or Toynbee.

Shortly afterward I began to think of a book called *The Rise and Fall of the Great Powers.* Published in 1987, it covered a mere five hundred years (1500 to 2000), but it attempted to look at the fate of all the great nations of that time. A few years later I wrote *Preparing for the Twenty-first Century* (1993), which essentially posed Barraclough's question anew by asking, What are the very largest changes taking place on our planet as we enter a new century? More recently I have written a book on the past, present, and future of the United Nations, which sounds more modest in scope, perhaps, but is a topic with enormous ramifications.

I still enjoy writing diplomatic, naval, and military history. But there is no doubt that a great part of me changed, some three or more decades ago, when I first picked up a book entitled *An Introduction to Contemporary History.*

PAUL KENNEDY is the J. Richardson Dilworth Professor of History and the director of International Security Studies at Yale University. In addition to the titles mentioned above, his works include *Strategy and Diplomacy*, *The Rise and Fall of British Naval Mastery*, *The Rise of the Anglo-German Antagonism*, and (as editor) *Grand Strategies in War and Peace* and *The War Plans of the Great Powers.* In 2000, Queen Elizabeth II named him Commander, Order of the British Empire, for his lifetime achievement in contemporary history. His book on the United Nations, *Parliament of Man*, was published by Random House in June 2006.

Collected Stories

Ernest Hemingway

Tracy Kidder

At some point during my first year at college, I discovered Hemingway. Within a few weeks, I think, I had read everything of his in print. He had killed himself only a couple of years before, and his heirs hadn't yet managed to find and publish all the half-baked manuscripts he'd left behind, so it was the uncorrupted oeuvre that I read. Still, I suspect I liked his best novels more than I should have, especially *A Farewell to Arms.* I don't want to reread any of them now, for fear of finding they have aged as gracelessly as I have. I do reread Hemingway's *Collected Stories,* though, with pleasure and admiration, and also with nostalgia.

I can't sort out what was real and what was fake in my late-adolescent responses to the best of those stories. I do think I decided to become a writer because I wanted to be a romantic figure like Hemingway. He introduced me to the idea of the writer as himself a hero. It would be unfair, of course, to blame him for the fact that I went to Vietnam as a soldier, but not entirely unfair to blame him for some of the romantic notions that were rattling around in my head when I went. At its best, his prose is far from simple, but to me it made the writing part of being a writer seem like the easy part. Once you'd performed heroic deeds—or, for the time being, imagined yourself performing them—you just told your story in declarative sentences strung together with lots of *and*s. No Latinate or multisyllabic words. Crisp dialogue, as elliptical as possible; a hero never confessed to his wounds. Hemingway's short stories were easy to imitate. Even today, I believe, young writers could find much worse places to start.

TRACY KIDDER is the author of *The Soul of a New Machine*, which won the Pulitzer Prize and the National Book Award. Widely recognized as a master of the nonfiction form, he has also written many other acclaimed books, including *House*, *Among Schoolchildren*, *Old Friends*, and *Mountains Beyond Mountains: The Quest of Dr. Paul Farmer, a Man Who Would Cure the World*. He was born in New York City, graduated from Harvard, and served in Vietnam for a year, an experience he chronicled in the recent memoir *My Detachment*. He lives in Massachusetts and Maine.

The Denial of Death

ERNEST BECKER

ROBERT KURSON

During a series of insomniac nights as a college sophomore, I pondered what it meant to be dead. The idea of not existing, and worse, not existing forever, was terrifying in ways daytime thoughts never can be. Would it be silent? Cold? Lonely? It seemed too much for the mind to grasp. I got to wondering how people walked around every day with equanimity when such a gargantuan and terrible and inescapable fate awaited.

A few days later, I happened across a paperback in the University of Wisconsin bookstore. Its title, *The Denial of Death*, grabbed me immediately. I plopped down on an old black leather chair and started reading. By the time I got up, I viewed the world differently. By the time I got up, I was a different person.

The book, written by cultural anthropologist Ernest Becker, is a brilliantly conceived and beautifully written synthesis of the thinking of Freud, Otto Rank, Kierkegaard, and other giant minds. It addresses what Becker thinks to be the basis for much of human culture, behavior, and character: man's refusal to acknowledge his own mortality. The reality of our fate, Becker argues, is too much for the human animal to bear; much of the world around us, from art to war to love to hate, from the forming of individual personalities to the construction of civilizations, arises from our desperate and usually unconscious efforts to deny our impermanence, to run from our animal doom.

I read *The Denial of Death* three times that year, and have read it many more times since. In it, I find answers to nearly every question I can think to ask about being human and about being in the world. In it, I find explanation for why men do what they do. It may sound odd to suggest that there is comfort to be found in a book about knowing our own mortality, but that is the beauty of Becker, and his gift is to show us that it is the beauty of ourselves.

After earning a bachelor's degree in philosophy from the University of Wisconsin and a law degree from Harvard, ROBERT KURSON left a career in real estate law to pursue writing. He was hired by the *Chicago Sun-Times* as a data-entry clerk, a job that led to a full-time position as a features writer. From the *Sun-Times* he moved to *Chicago* magazine, and then to *Esquire*, where he is a contributing editor. He is the author of *Shadow Divers*, and his award-winning stories have appeared in *Rolling Stone*, *The New York Times Magazine*, and other publications. He lives in the Chicago suburbs and can be reached via the Internet at robert@robertkurson.com.

To Kill a Mockingbird

HARPER LEE

HARPER LEE AND JULIA PEASE

WALLY LAMB

I knew from the time I was eight that I wanted to be a teacher, but not that I wanted to be a writer. In third grade, my lowest marks were in reading ("Walter needs to check out more library books") and writing ("Walter needs to practice his penmanship and be less sloppy"). If you'd suggested to my teacher, prim Miss Comstock, that I'd grow up to be a novelist, she might have thrown back her head and guffawed.

My eighth-grade English teacher, Mrs. Cramer, took us outside to write about nature (which I liked) and made us memorize her favorite poems (which I didn't). Longfellow's "Evangeline," Joyce Kilmer's "Trees," Vachel Lindsay's "The Potato's Dance": none of these works spoke to me, and anyway, what kind of men had first names like Vachel and Joyce? At a schoolwide assembly, our class was made to mount the gymnasium stage and recite, in unison, "The Potato's Dance." I'd been tapped for a solo quatrain that required me to step to the front of the stage and speak the following lines, which I still remember at age fifty-five, possibly because of posttraumatic stress syndrome.

> There was just one sweet potato.
> He was golden-brown and slim:

The lady loved his figure.
She danced all night with him.

As I spoke, I could see the science teachers snickering at the rear of the gym. I forgave them immediately. I thought literature was kind of stupid too.

Later that school year, President Kennedy got killed. Then Beatlemania happened. Then it was eighth-grade graduation. I was only half paying attention when Miss Higgins, the scary teacher at the microphone, called my name. I got off my folding chair and took the perp walk to the front of the auditorium. Miss Higgins handed me an envelope. On the outside it said, "Julia Pease Award for Writing." Inside was a crisp ten-dollar bill. A writing award? For me? As I returned to my seat, Mrs. Cramer's wink implied that there had not been a mistake. But later that day at Ocean Beach Park, I spent all my prize money on Skee-Ball and mini-golf, just in case.

In high school, I read and wrote because I had to, not because I wanted to. In English, a book report was coming due. I was a poky reader who favored short books for these assignments, but I'd already reported on Orwell's *Animal Farm* and Steinbeck's *The Red Pony.* From my sister's nightstand, I grabbed the paperback she'd been yapping about, *To Kill a Mockingbird.* The cover had a Technicolor picture of Gregory Peck and some little girl in overalls. I opened the book and read the first sentence: "When he was nearly thirteen, my brother Jem got his arm badly broken at the elbow." Three days later, I finished the book. A novel had never kidnapped me before. Until *Mockingbird*, I'd had no idea that literature could exert so strong a power.

Like its progenitor, Twain's *The Adventures of Huckleberry Finn*, and its big brother, Salinger's *The Catcher in the Rye*, Harper Lee's *To Kill a Mockingbird* is a first-person narrative in which conscience is tested and hypocrisy is skewered. There's neighborhood intrigue, a rape trial, the attempted murder of innocents, and laugh-out-loud comic relief. The narrator, a sadder but wiser adult, gives the floor early and often to the child's voice and viewpoint. The reader gets all this good stuff, plus Lee's sensual and evocative language. Listen to how she describes a Depression-era town in the Deep South.

> Somehow, it was hotter then: a black dog suffered on a summer's day; bony mules hitched to Hoover carts flicked flies in the sweltering shade of the live oaks on the square. Men's stiff collars wilted by nine in the morning. Ladies bathed before noon, after their three-o'clock naps, and by nightfall were like soft teacakes with frostings of sweat and sweet talcum.

Pass me a sweat towel and a sweet tea, Miss Harper. It's summertime and I'm in Alabama.

In college, I fell in love with other fictions: Fitzgerald's *The Great Gatsby*, Cather's *My Ántonia*, Dreiser's *Sister Carrie.* In grad school, it was the masters of the short story form who captured my heart: Flannery O'Connor, John Updike, Raymond Carver, Andre Dubus. But like they say, there's something special about your first.

A native of Norwich, Connecticut, WALLY LAMB is the best-selling author of two novels, *She's Come Undone* and *I Know This Much Is True*, both New York Times Notable Books and selections of Oprah's Book Club. Among his many honors are the Pushcart Prize, the Connecticut Governor's Arts Award, and the Kenneth Johnson Memorial Book Award, which recognized *I Know This Much Is True* for its contribution to destigmatizing mental illness. Lamb taught high school and university students for twenty-five years, and for the past six years has served as volunteer facilitator of a writing workshop at a maximum-security women's prison in Niantic, Connecticut.

From this program came *Couldn't Keep It to Myself: Testimonies from Our Imprisoned Sisters*, an anthology of autobiographical essays by his inmate students, which he edited and introduced. He is currently at work on his third novel, *The Hour I First Believed*. He and his wife, Christine, are the parents of three sons: Jared, Justin, and Teddy.

The Only Dance There Is
RAM DASS

and more

ANNE LAMOTT

It's so hard to pick one book. I'll tell you a few of the books that gave me faith, direction, and most of all a sense that there were other odd, magical, sensitive, lonely people just like me in the world; that there was in fact connection and community, if you just found the right writers.

Reading *Pippi Longstocking* when I was seven gave me a new lease on life. I felt pretty homely and different, and Pippi was so out there, with her freckles and upside-down braids, one black sock and one brown. She was so feisty and hilarious and powerful. I wanted her to be my best friend, and I also knew that she lived inside me. That was such a great secret—that inside me I was okay if Pippi was. I wanted to grow up and tell stories like hers, about girls who kicked *butt.* I loved *Little Women* for the same reason. Oh, Jo—thank you, God, for Jo.

I read Langston Hughes in seventh grade, and was never the same again. People had always thought I was half black because of my nappy hair and heavy-lidded eyes, and when I read Langston Hughes, I really wanted to be. I identified with the people in his poetry, and was hungry to experience his love for them, his pride in them, his passion and encouragement of their truth and values.

Gather out of star-dust
Earth-dust,
Cloud-dust,
Storm-dust,
And splinters of hail,
One handful of dream-dust
Not for sale.

No one had ever spoken to me like this before.

When I was eighteen, I read Kierkegaard's *Fear and Trembling* with a great Czechoslovakian feminist professor at Goucher College, and I had my first non-stoned true and direct spiritual experience. I understood suddenly that faith was not sweet and Hallmark-card poetic, but a deep-core, heartbreaking, cellular decision, made in the dark and the weirdness and the wound. The book shook me up so much that it made me a little crazy, which is an excellent thing in this society.

When I was about twenty, I read *The Only Dance There Is*, a book of lectures given by Ram Dass at the Menninger Foundation and Spring Grove Hospital, about consciousness, God, spirit, his own hilarious and neurotic inner life. The lectures were addressed to the other spiritual seekers in the audience, who I believe were psychiatrists and psychologists working with the quote-unquote mentally ill. The book begins this way: "Last evening, here in Topeka, as one of the journeyers on a path, a very, very old path, the path of consciousness, I, in a sense, met with the Explorers Club to tell about the geography I had been mapping." Ram Dass's book was incredibly funny and profound, and it threw the lights on for me. It freed me from my fear of being seen as a seeker, because it freed me from the belief that religious and spiritual people were dull and preachy assholes. It was a book about how he was seeking to be both deeply human and immersed in the truth of our spiritual identity. It was about community, loss, resurrection, other realities, his teachers, his family, his own empty, rich, precious self.

I knew the day I read *The Only Dance There Is* that this was what I was going to do with my life: pursue spiritual truth, and try to help people laugh as part of their healing path. Finding that book taught me a lesson about how truth comes to us in such quirky, unexpected packages, because it was one of the worst days of my life. It was Easter Sunday, probably in 1974, and I was lying in my adorable hippie boyfriend's bed with the stomach flu, and he had gone to be with his *other* girlfriend, what with us all being so hip and all, and me not being much of a date for Easter dinner. When he left, I really felt like I would die from being so sick and alone and jealous. Then I picked up this book he'd been reading, and I felt like it was worth any price to feel so guided, understood, trusted, and entertained, all at once. My soul was so hungry and thirsty for Ram Dass's voice that I read the book in one sitting—or rather, in one lying, because I was sick in bed. I remember drinking this disgusting herbal tea all day—chaparral tea, which tastes like couch stuffing—because there wasn't anything else in his house. When I was done, I washed my face, brushed my teeth, put the book down by the side of the bed, and left. It was a great day.

ANNE LAMOTT is the author of six novels, most recently *Blue Shoe*, and four works of nonfiction, including *Bird by Bird* and *Plan B: Further Thoughts on Faith*. She lives in northern California with her son, Sam.

The Interpretation of Dreams

SIGMUND FREUD

BARBARA LEAMING

Most of the books I have loved have been novels.

I think I could be perfectly happy marooned on a desert island with Anthony Trollope's Palliser novels and *The Way We Live Now.* And I will never be "finished" with Henry James' *The Golden Bowl* or Edith Wharton's *The House of Mirth.* Tolstoy's *War and Peace* and *Anna Karenina* and Gogol's *Dead Souls* are stacked atop one another next to my bed, always ready to hand. These are books that have given me great pleasure and sustenance as I read and reread them through the years, yet I cannot really say that any one of them changed my life.

Curiously, the book that altered everything for me was Sigmund Freud's *The Interpretation of Dreams.*

It was not any aspect of Freud's psychological theories per se that had such a massive impact on me when I first read *The Interpretation of Dreams* as a very young woman. Instead, it was the way in which he treated a dream as a narrative—a story put together by the dreamer, which Freud then proceeded to take apart for purposes of understanding. In breaking down particular dreams to their component parts and showing how those parts were linked to one another, Freud taught me to see narrative structure as I simply had never done before.

By prompting me to think about how narratives work, *The Interpretation of Dreams* made me want to be a writer.

BARBARA LEAMING is the author of biographies of Orson Welles and Katharine Hepburn, among others. Her most recent book is *Jack Kennedy: The Education of a Statesman*.

The Bible

Senator Joe Lieberman

The book that changed my life? The temptation is to say: "All of them!" I can't think of a book, fiction or nonfiction—even books I didn't like—that didn't add something to my life. Every time you read and learn something new, or read something that challenges what you thought you knew, your life is changed dramatically over time as you continue learning and thinking.

There is also a magic in reading. Books have taken me to places I never thought I would visit, introduced me to people I never thought I would meet, and transported me to times past and futures imagined I never thought I would experience.

But taking the question in its most titanic form, I would have to say the Bible is "the book that changed my life." I am a religiously observant Jew whose life has been shaped by the faith and commandments contained in the Bible.

The Bible is powerful reading. Take the opening sentence, Genesis 1:1—"In the beginning God created the heaven and the earth." That has to rank as one of the best openings in the history of books. In a simple declarative sentence of just ten words, the reader's most fundamental questions about life—How did I get here?—are answered.

While the Bible is the book that has had the most profound effect on my life, there are many authors whose books have helped shape me at different ages.

As a child, I loved the books of William Saroyan for their faraway ethnic richness, idealism, and humanity.

Theodore White's *The Making of the President, 1960* deepened my admiration for John F. Kennedy and intensified my interest in politics.

William Manchester's biography of Winston Churchill drew me to a man of political integrity and courage who helped protect and shape the modern civilized world.

Robert Penn Warren's *All the King's Men* may be the best American novel about politics and power. The tragedy of the novel's central character, Willie Stark, rivals Shakespeare's *Macbeth* as a cautionary tale about the dangers of power without purpose—power sought merely for its own sake, with all ideals forsaken in pursuit of that goal.

Finally, I have been enriched by just about everything by Mark Twain. His novels, short stories, and essays still ring true a century later in both their humor and insight into the human condition. Twain is a fantastic writer because he makes it look so easy—like a great athlete. But anyone who has tried to write, as I have, knows how hard Twain worked.

Let me close with a Twain thought on reading, from *The Prince and the Pauper.* "When I am king, they shall not have bread and shelter only, but also teachings out of books, for a full belly is little worth where the mind is starved."

Now in his third term representing Connecticut in the U.S. Senate, JOE LIEBERMAN is ranking member of the Homeland Security and Governmental Affairs Committee, and a member of the Environment and Public Works Committee, the Senate Armed Services Committee, and the Small Business Committee. He is the author, with Michael D'Orso, of *In Praise of Public Life*, and with his wife, Hadassah, of *An Amazing*

Adventure: Joe and Hadassah's Personal Notes on the 2000 Campaign, a chronicle of his vice-presidential run. He and Hadassah live in New Haven and Washington. They are the proud parents of four children, and the proud grandparents of three.

Jane Eyre

CHARLOTTE BRONTË

MARGOT LIVESEY

When I was nine, my father announced that we were moving from the isolated Scottish boys' school where he had taught for all of my life, and much of his, to another school in a small village in the Borders of Scotland. The two schools, I discovered later, were only a little more than a hundred miles apart, but in our ancient car the journey took most of a day. I remember sitting in the backseat, daydreaming about my large new life; in the comics I read, girls were always going out into the world, making friends and having adventures. And after living in the remote countryside, I was thrilled by the prospect of a village, with shops and neighbors.

Barely a week passed, however, before I found myself unbearably lonely. My elderly father and my elderly stepmother were absorbed in their adult worlds, and my one reliable companion, the family dog, was afraid of noise and traffic. What use were all these neighbors when I was unable to get to know them? In the midst of those difficult days, a book in my father's bookcase caught my eye because it had a girl's name on the spine.

From the opening chapter, where Jane Eyre is unjustly punished by her unkind aunt, I was entirely on her side. She was small, plain, and friendless. She was not especially talented. She was appealingly passionate; so passionate indeed that only much later, when I taught the novel, did I notice that both Jane and her author, Charlotte Brontë, seem entirely unaware of sex.

Reading about Jane's adventures didn't change my life in any of the ways I hoped—neither Helen Burns nor Rochester appeared to keep me company—but the book did show me that life is change. Like Jane's, my life had changed for the worse, and like hers, it could also change for the better. Time would, irrevocably, carry me to a new place.

For years I assumed that my profound identification with Jane Eyre had to do with the similarities in our situations, but recently I found myself discussing the novel with an Englishman in his eighties and an American in his fifties. The Englishman described how he had read *Jane Eyre* during the Burma campaign in the Second World War and missed an important landing because Rochester was about to propose. The American described sitting in Washington Square Park in New York, reading the chapter where Jane nearly dies after she leaves Rochester, and being transported. *Jane Eyre* speaks to the secret, vulnerable part of ourselves that has little to do with age or gender or race or situation. As I sat under the blackcurrant bushes in our garden, turning those pages, I recognized that part of myself and felt recognized in turn. That recognition changed my life.

MARGOT LIVESEY was born and grew up on the edge of the Scottish Highlands. After taking a B.A. in literature and philosophy at the University of York in England, she spent most of her twenties in Toronto writing and waitressing. Subsequently she moved to the United States, where she has taught at Williams College and the Iowa Writers' Workshop, among other schools and programs. She has received grants from the National Endowment for the Arts and the Guggenheim Foundation, and is the author of a collection of stories and five novels, including *Criminals*, *Eva Moves the Furniture*, and most recently *Banishing Verona*. She now lives mostly in Boston, where she is a writer in residence at Emerson College.

For Whom the Bell Tolls

ERNEST HEMINGWAY

SENATOR JOHN McCAIN

One auspicious day when I was twelve years old, I found two four-leaf clovers in our front yard. Cupping my tokens of good fortune, I ran excitedly into the house, entered my father's study, and grabbed from his shelves the first book that came to hand. I opened it and carefully placed the clovers between its pages. Many hours passed before I reluctantly closed it.

I had opened *For Whom the Bell Tolls* at the tenth chapter. The pages that had seized my attention offered a stark and gripping portrait of inhumanity. The leader of a band of guerrillas fighting on the Republican side in the Spanish Civil War orders his men to round up the local gentry of a small town, beat them to death, and throw their bodies over a cliff. Riveting stuff to a twelve-year-old boy. I took the book to my room, finished reading the chapter, turned to the first page, and read straight through to the end in one sitting. From that day on, Ernest Hemingway was my favorite author and *For Whom the Bell Tolls* was my favorite book.

What moved me so was more than the brutality of war depicted in the author's spare and elegant style. I idolized the story's hero, Robert Jordan, the idealistic college professor from Montana who comes to Spain to fight fascists, grows disillusioned with the leaders of his cause and the cynical outside forces that influence them, and despairs of the futility of his last mission, to blow up a bridge that holds little military value. But he falls in love at first sight with the beautiful Maria, whose parents have been murdered and she terribly abused by the fascists, and in the last three days of his life he is transformed by his love, and recognizes the real cause for which he is prepared to sacrifice his life. He is not fighting for politicians. He is not fighting for a form of government or a socioeconomic order. He is fighting for people he has come to love, because he can find no honor or happiness in remaining apart from human suffering.

Of course, *For Whom the Bell Tolls* is full of adventure and fighting and romance, to which my child's intellect responded more readily than to its moral. And by the end, with my hero having sacrificed his life to save his love, I considered the book mostly a lesson on how a great man should live and die—a great man must always be his own man, and have the courage for it, and he must die with style.

In the moment before his death, Jordan thinks to himself, "The world is a fine place and worth the fighting for and I hate very much to leave it." To me the line was as perfect as a Psalm, although I doubt I understood its full import. Brave men uttered such things when they died, I thought, if they had style as well as courage. Robert Jordan died proving that no man is an island, but by the time I completely grasped his meaning, many years had passed, much of a lifetime, in fact, since the day when a stroke of very good luck led me to his story.

U.S. Senator JOHN MCCAIN graduated from the Naval Academy in 1958 and served with distinction as a naval aviator. He was elected to Congress in 1982, representing what was then the first congressional district of Arizona, and to the Senate in 1986. Currently the senior senator from Arizona, he is chairman of the Senate Committee on Indian Affairs, and serves on the Armed Services Committee and the Commerce,

Science, and Transportation Committee. Senator McCain is the author of three books (with Mark Salter), *Character Is Destiny*, *Why Courage Matters*, and *Faith of My Fathers*. He has seven children and four grandchildren, and lives in Phoenix with his wife, Cindy.

Henry VIII

William Shakespeare

Frank McCourt

The other two beds in my room at the Fever Hospital are empty. The nurse says I'm the only typhoid patient and I'm a miracle for getting over the crisis.

The room next to me is empty till one morning a girl's voice says, Yoo hoo, who's there?

I'm not sure if she's talking to me or someone in the room beyond.

Yoo hoo, boy with the typhoid, are you awake?

I am.

Are you better?

I am.

Well, why are you here?

I don't know. I'm still in the bed. They stick needles in me and give me medicine.

What do you look like?

I wonder, What kind of a question is that? I don't know what to tell her.

Yoo hoo, are you there, typhoid boy?

I am.

What's your name?

Frank.

That's a good name. My name is Patricia Madigan. How old are you?

Ten.

Oh. She sounds disappointed.

But I'll be eleven in August, next month.

Well, that's better than ten. I'll be fourteen in September. Do you want to know why I'm in the Fever Hospital?

I do.

I have diphtheria and something else.

What's something else?

They don't know. They think I have a disease from foreign parts because my father used to be in Africa. I nearly died. Are you going to tell me what you look like?

I have black hair.

You and millions.

I have brown eyes with bits of green that's called hazel.

You and thousands.

I have stitches on the back of my right hand and my two feet where they put in the soldier's blood.

Oh, God, did they?

They did.

You won't be able to stop marching and saluting.

There's a swish of habit and click of beads and then Sister Rita's voice. Now, now, what's this? There's to be no talking between two rooms especially when it's a boy and a girl. Do you hear me, Patricia?

I do, Sister.

Do you hear me, Francis?

I do, Sister.

You could be giving thanks for your two remarkable recoveries. You could be saying the rosary. You could be reading *The Little Messenger of the Sacred Heart* that's beside your beds. Don't let me come back and find you talking.

She comes into my room and wags her finger at me. Especially you, Francis, after thousands of boys prayed for you at the Confraternity. Give thanks, Francis, give thanks.

She leaves and there's silence for awhile. Then Patricia whispers, Give thanks, Francis, give thanks, and say your rosary, Francis, and I laugh so hard a nurse runs in to see if I'm all right. She's a very stern nurse from the County Kerry and she frightens me. What's this, Francis? Laughing? What is there to laugh about? Are you and that Madigan girl talking? I'll report you to Sister Rita. There's to be no laughing for you could be doing serious damage to your internal apparatus.

She plods out and Patricia whispers again in a heavy Kerry accent, No laughing, Francis, you could be doin' serious damage to your internal apparatus. Say your rosary, Francis, and pray for your internal apparatus.

Mam visits me on Thursdays. I'd like to see my father, too, but I'm out of danger, crisis time is over, and I'm allowed only one visitor. Besides, she says, he's back at work at Rank's Flour Mills and please God this job will last a while with the war on and the English desperate for flour. She brings me a chocolate bar and that proves Dad is working. She could never afford it on the dole. He sends me notes. He tells me my brothers are all praying for me, that I should be a good boy, obey the doctors, the nuns, the nurses, and don't forget to say my prayers. He's sure St. Jude pulled me through the crisis because he's the patron saint of desperate cases and I was indeed a desperate case.

Patricia says she has two books by her bed. One is a poetry book and that's the one she loves. The other is a short history of England and do I want it? She gives it to Seamus, the man who mops the floors every day, and he brings it to me. He says, I'm not supposed to be bringing anything from a dipteria room to a typhoid room with all the germs flying around and hiding between the pages and if you ever catch dipteria on top of the typhoid they'll know and I'll lose my good job and be out on the street singing patriotic songs with a tin cup in my hand, which I could easily do because there isn't a song ever written about

Ireland's sufferings I don't know and a few songs about the joy of whiskey too.

Oh, yes, he knows Roddy McCorley. He'll sing it for me right enough but he's barely into the first verse when the Kerry nurse rushes in. What's this, Seamus? Singing? Of all the people in this hospital you should know the rules against singing. I have a good mind to report you to Sister Rita.

Ah, God, don't do that, nurse.

Very well, Seamus. I'll let it go this one time. You know the singing could lead to a relapse in these patients.

When she leaves he whispers he'll teach me a few songs because singing is good for passing the time when you're by yourself in a typhoid room. He says Patricia is a lovely girl the way she often gives him sweets from the parcel her mother sends every fortnight. He stops mopping the floor and calls to Patricia in the next room, I was telling Frankie you're a lovely girl, Patricia, and she says, You're a lovely man, Seamus. He smiles because he's an old man of forty and he never had children but the ones he can talk to here in the Fever Hospital. He says, Here's the book, Frankie. Isn't it a great pity you have to be reading all about England after all they did to us, that there isn't a history of Ireland to be had in this hospital.

The book tells me all about King Alfred and William the Conqueror and all the kings and queens down to Edward, who had to wait forever for his mother, Victoria, to die before he could be king. The book has the first bit of Shakespeare I ever read.

I do believe, induced by potent circumstances
That thou art mine enemy.

The history writer says this is what Catherine, who is a wife of Henry the Eighth, says to Cardinal Wolsey, who is trying to have her head cut off. I don't know what it means and I don't care because it's Shakespeare and it's like having jewels in my mouth when I say the words. If I had a whole book of Shakespeare they could keep me in the hospital for a year.

FRANK McCOURT was born in Brooklyn in 1930, to immigrant parents who took the family back to Ireland when he was four. His first book, *Angela's Ashes*, a memoir of his childhood in the slums of Limerick, won the Pulitzer Prize, the National Book Critics Circle Award, and the Los Angeles Times Book Prize. He is also the author of *'Tis*, which recounts his harrowing experiences after he came back to America in 1949, and *Teacher Man*, a memoir of his thirty years teaching English in New York City high schools. He and his wife, Ellen, live in New York and Connecticut.

The Great Gatsby

F. Scott Fitzgerald

Faith Middleton

On the morning of my first college class in the late sixties, Professor Hildegarde Cummings, a tall, full-figured woman who favored sensible shoes, introduced herself to us by noting that she was oddly talented at judging competitive figure skaters on television, even though she had no skating experience.

She had our undivided attention: the idea that any of us might be mysteriously sensational at something was irresistible. As she spoke the opening line of an Emily Dickinson poem, "I heard a Fly buzz—when I died," I knew how lucky I was to be in college, a place I had spent exactly no time imagining as a high school student in Connecticut.

During my sophomore year of high school, I lost both of my Scottish immigrant parents, who left me with a generalized sense of ambition lacking a particular target. That is, until I found myself in an English class taught by Hugh Boyle, a statuesque man who was partial to perfectly tailored tweed suits worn always with bow ties. On the first day of class, Mr. Boyle passed out copies of *The Great Gatsby*, a novel by a man none of us had ever heard of, F. Scott Fitzgerald.

Each evening, at my older sister's home, where I now lived, I fell into Gatsby's world and never wanted to leave. I was mesmerized by Fitzgerald's timeless story, set in the 1920s Jazz Age, a period of roaring prosperity and materialism. And each morning, Mr. Boyle steered us into debates about money and class and what makes a good novel. Something shifted in me then, the way the narrow highway out of Denver opens suddenly at Kenosha Pass, revealing breathtaking vistas as far as the eye can see. Just like that, my future had detail. It was F. Scott Fitzgerald who made me want to go to college.

Some time ago, the Sunday *New York Times* ran all of *The Great Gatsby* in weekly installments. I was delighted by the communal spirit of the paper's summer project, and I hoped that somewhere among the readers was a teenager who might glimpse for the first time what a world is out there.

FAITH MIDDLETON, a two-time recipient of the Peabody Award, is host and executive producer of *The Faith Middleton Show* on WNPR, and author of *The Goodness of Ordinary People: True Stories from Real Americans.*

A Tree Grows in Brooklyn

BETTY SMITH

JACQUELYN MITCHARD

I must have been twelve, or perhaps a little older, when I first read *A Tree Grows in Brooklyn,* by Betty Smith. It was then considered a rather benign middle schooler's book, even though its portrayal of immigrant poverty—including death from alcoholism, a case of pedophilia, and soul-searching about premarital sex—is much more gritty and heart-wrenching even than Frank McCourt's *Angela's Ashes,* written half a century later. The sheer honesty and simple eloquence of Smith's storytelling riveted my adolescent mind, and the relationship between Francie Nolan and her gallant, practical mother recapitulated my own urban upbringing as a plumber's daughter, the first person in her family ever to graduate from high school. Our situation in our west-side Chicago apartment was never so desperate. But when I grew up and began to write, I approached my own stories differently from my friends who had multiple degrees in creative writing. I wrote from the perspective of a blue-collar girl; and I wrote about ordinary people. And I always will.

When my first novel, *The Deep End of the Ocean*, was published to some acclaim two years after I was widowed, I adopted a baby daughter. I named her Francie Nolan, because she put me in mind of what Betty Smith said about the tree of the title, the luxuriant weed called the Tree of Heaven: that it would be beautiful except that there were so many like it. There were many like my Francie, and I couldn't change all their futures.

But I could change just this one. And I also believed Francie would need to struggle up through the cracks in the concrete, without many material advantages, without a father's staunch love.

In fact, my Francie—just like Laurie Nolan McShane, the baby in Betty Smith's novel—did find a wonderful father, literally when he walked up onto our porch to do some artful handmade tiling. We'd known each other less than one month before we decided to marry, and that was seven years ago. On my next birthday, my agent gave me a present, a first edition of *A Tree Grows in Brooklyn.* What I didn't know, and I'm not sure that she or the bookseller did either, was that tucked among the pages were letters from Smith to her own agent, written just before the publication of the novel and the simultaneous tumult about the upcoming film. Betty Smith lived in a house on Post Road then. So did I. She'd just met the love of her life, and she married within weeks of their meeting, just as I had.

Each time I sit down to begin a novel, I read "my book" again. I take from it lessons in writing, courage, and the absolutely intransigent necessity for utter honesty. Perhaps because of who I am, and from whence I came, nothing else between two covers has ever meant more to me.

JACQUELYN MITCHARD's first novel, *The Deep End of the Ocean*, was the first selection of Oprah's Book Club. She is the author of six other novels—*The Most Wanted*; *A Theory of Relativity*; *Twelve Times Blessed*; *Christmas, Present*; *The Breakdown Lane*; and most recently *Cage of Stars*—as well as three books for children, an essay collection, *The Rest of Us: Dispatches from the Mother Ship*, and two works of nonfiction, *Mother Less Child: The Love Story of a Family* and *Jane Addams.* Her syndicated column for Tribune Media Services appears in 128 newspapers nationwide, and her essays on parenthood and social issues have been widely anthologized. A recipient of the Maggie Award for Public Service Magazine Journalism, she was a speech-writer for Donna Shalala, former secretary of Health and Human Services, and was a finalist for Britain's Orange Prize and a fiction juror for the 2002 National Book Awards. She lives in Wisconsin with her husband, Christopher Brent, and their seven children.

The 87th Precinct Series

Ed McBain

Leigh Montville

The 87th Precinct closed for business in the summer of last year. The death of novelist Evan Hunter/Ed McBain at the age of seventy-eight brought an end to a place I had frequented for more than thirty years, a fictional environment that had become as familiar as my hometown, populated by people who were closer to me than most of my present neighbors.

I was surprised at how deeply I felt the loss. I wanted to attend a wake for McBain's characters, a graveside service for Detective Steve Carella, for Meyer Meyer and Bert Kling, and even for Fat Ollie Weeks, the resident bigot and numbskull. This was the end of a universe, a mudslide of epic proportions, a disaster, everyone wiped out at once.

Strange, huh?

I was in my early twenties when the sportswriter in the next cubicle at *The Boston Globe* suggested that I "check out the books of this Ed McBain guy." I checked and never stopped checking. Through a couple of marriages, four or five houses, a few career swerves, and the long process of raising two children to adulthood, I made at least two stops every year in the world created by this one writer under his two pen names.

He was a prolific son of a gun. He wrote fifty-five books about the 87th Precinct alone. He wrote twenty-one more with other characters under the McBain pseudonym, twenty-five as Evan Hunter. He wrote a dozen or so books under still other names, ten collections of short stories, four children's books, four screenplays, and two plays.

The constant through all this was solid declarative writing, wonderful plots, and at least six observations or turns of phrase per book that set off many bells and whistles in a quiet room. If a reader climbed through all one hundred and thirty or so published works at an average of two and a half days per book—and I haven't, but I have read a bunch—that would be nearly a year's worth of enjoyment.

Let's say the first book of McBain's I read was *Fuzz* or *Doll* or *Ax*. A year's worth of enjoyment is a pretty good change in anyone's life.

LEIGH MONTVILLE, formerly a sports columnist at *The Boston Globe* and senior writer at *Sports Illustrated,* is the author of *At the Altar of Speed: The Fast Life and Tragic Death of Dale Earnhardt* and *Ted Williams: The Biography of an American Hero*, both *New York Times* bestsellers. His most recent book is *The Big Bam: The Life and Times of Babe Ruth.*

Marjorie Morningstar

HERMAN WOUK

Compromising Positions

SUSAN ISAACS

SARA NELSON

The book that changed my life? Well, actually, there were two—one that seriously altered the way I thought about reading, and one that influenced me as a writer.

The first was *Marjorie Morningstar*, Herman Wouk's 1955 novel about a Jewish girl growing up in New York on the eve of World War II. It lives so large in my memory because it was the first adult book my mother (who, by the way, was a Jewish girl who'd grown up in New York on the eve of World War II) ever pressed on me. I was about thirteen, and up until then I'd read what would now be called YA novels, along with the occasional "worthy" book that was assigned as homework. (There was a flap at my not too progressive school, I remember, when a forward-thinking science teacher had the eighth grade read Huxley's *Brave New World*.) So I didn't really know that there was such a thing as popular fiction that actually had something to say. Of course, at the time, all I cared about was the love story between this princess and the non-Jewish renegade prince her parents despised—like I said, I was thirteen—and it wasn't until I reread *Marjorie Morningstar* recently that I saw how powerfully this "popular" novel spoke to classic themes like identity and belonging.

The second book that influenced me is also very "light," but like *Marjorie Morningstar*, it changed the way I think about what reading and literature are supposed to be. That book was Susan Isaacs' *Compromising Positions*, a hilarious whodunit about a Long Island housewife circa 1975 who gets caught up in investigating the murder of a local dentist. If I could stand the words, I'd use "feisty" or "sassy" to describe Isaacs' characters and writing and point of view; at the time, all I thought was, Gee, maybe someday I could write something this smart and funny.

And maybe someday I will.

SARA NELSON became editor in chief of *Publishers Weekly* in January 2005, after a stint as the Book Beat columnist for the *New York Post*. A journalist for twenty-five years, she has written for *The New York Observer*, *The New York Times*, *The Wall Street Journal*, and many national magazines. She is the author of the Book Sense bestseller *So Many Books, So Little Time*, a memoir and reading guide, and has taught at the Radcliffe Publishing Course, the NYU Summer Publishing Institute, and the Columbia Graduate School of Journalism. She lives in New York City.

Ab the Cave Man

WILLIAM LEWIS NIDA

SHERWIN B. NULAND

I was seven years old when I had the transformative experience of seeing my name on a brand-new library card. The very first volume I took out at the Kingsbridge Branch of the New York Public Library in the Bronx had a title as unforgettable as the effect the book itself would have on me. *Ab the Cave Man* changed my notion of what the printed word could do. Until then, my contact with reading had been the cloying porridge of the classroom. I had no idea that reading could be fun, that a boy might be transported to another place and another time and become so engrossed by descriptions and characters that he lost all awareness of his surroundings, his worldly life, and the very hour of the day. From its opening sentences, *Ab the Cave Man* immersed me in an atmosphere unlike any I had ever known or even imagined.

I was a kid to whom no one at home had ever read. The adults in my family were immigrants whose means I would exaggerate were I to call them modest. Spoken English was difficult enough to deal with, and mastering words on a page had proven beyond the capacity of the limited attention they could pay to it in the midst of their struggles merely to survive in this confusing land. But the lesson of their failed example was clear—command of the language was the real passport to America and to the greater world of which I knew so little. To realize suddenly, with the first pages of this small maroon-covered miracle, that books were actually the stuff of which dreams are made was the revelation after which neither the English language nor the notion of narrative would ever be the same. Something previously undiscovered in my spirit was revealed by that little volume—it has influenced me every time I read and every time I pick up my pencil to write.

SHERWIN B. NULAND is the author of *How We Die: Reflections on Life's Final Chapter*, which won the National Book Award in 1994 and was a finalist for the Pulitzer Prize and the National Book Critics Circle Award. Among his other works are *How We Live*, *Leonardo da Vinci*, *Lost in America: A Journey with My Father*, and *Maimonides.* A clinical professor of surgery at the Yale School of Medicine and a fellow of the university's Institution for Social and Policy Studies, he has written extensively for such publications as *The New York Review of Books*, *Time*, *The New Republic*, *The New York Times*, and *The American Scholar.* He lives in Connecticut with his family.

Eloise

KAY THOMPSON

LAURA NUMEROFF

Boy oh boy! The book that changed my life! That would definitely have to be *Eloise* by Kay Thompson! I was nine years old and an avid book lover by then thanks to my parents. I remember opening *Eloise* for the first time and thinking it was very special because of the unusual layout of the text and illustrations. I liked Eloise's quirky looks and her poochy belly and winsome smile.

And then I started reading. It was different from any other book I'd read. It had run-on sentences with no periods! How could that be! It wasn't what we learned in school! Didn't Mrs. Thompson know any better? But I loved it all the more because it was Eloise talking and she was so funny.

And she lived in the Plaza Hotel in Manhattan! And I was from Brooklyn! And she ordered room service! And I had stayed in a motel and dreamed of room service! I was living vicariously through Eloise!

I couldn't put the book down. And soon I fell in love with Nanny and Skipperdee and Weenie too, and all of Eloise's antics and her running all over the Plaza, and oh my you just have to read the book for yourself but I think you get the picture because after I read it only a hundred gazillion times not only did it become my favorite book but I decided that I was rawther mad about creative writing and wanted to become an author just like Mrs. Thompson for Lord's sake! And not only did I become an author because of *Eloise*, but I am published by the same publisher, and I also got to meet the illustrator, Hilary Knight, twice! I almost fainted!

LAURA NUMEROFF is a *New York Times* bestselling author of thirty picture books for children, including *If You Give a Mouse a Cookie*, *If You Give a Moose a Muffin*, and *What Mommies Do Best/What Daddies Do Best*. She grew up in Brooklyn, New York, graduated from the Pratt Institute, and now resides in Los Angeles.

So Long, See You Tomorrow

William Maxwell

Stewart O'Nan

As a writer, I'm at the mercy of books. Because I have to live with them day to day, the ones I write necessarily change the way I see the world, charging me so I catch new associations and connections sparking off everything. I hope the ones I read will excite me the same way, moving me and letting me see the world from a new perspective.

It happens more often than you'd think, though mostly in ecstatic snatches, little bolts of insight. I'm jaded now, I'm sure, and occasionally self-absorbed, but it's a rare author who puts it together for a whole book.

William Maxwell does it for me in his last novel, *So Long, See You Tomorrow.* When I came to the book, I was thirty, and naturally looking back on my life—essentially what his retrospective narrator does, from the more forgiving perspective of old age. The novel opens in what might be called an intimate first person. A man Maxwell's age, who shares much of his biography, is recalling a strange murder in his small Illinois town back when he was a child, soon after the death of his mother during the flu outbreak of 1918. There's a warmth to the voice, and a wistfulness. The town and all the people in it are long gone, but the events, and the shameful way the narrator treated a boy he barely knew, compel him to remember.

Maxwell's narrator directly asks us to return with him and imagine how all this must have happened. Here he switches to the third person, recounting the lives of the murderer and his victim and the boy the narrator treated so badly—the son of the murderer. The characters hurt each other terribly, yet through the narrator's (or is it Maxwell's?) generosity, we come to feel deeply for all of them. For all the loss and sorrow, there is—strangely—something redemptive in the telling. Out of guilt and love, through the power of memory and empathy, Maxwell and his narrator memorialize and thereby save this lost world that meant so much to both of them.

Maxwell does this, and does it richly, in 135 pages. Technically the novel is brilliant, a miracle of compression and tone, but what moves me most is the narrator's ability to address the past and come to terms with his mistakes—to show us his shortcomings and in a way apologize for the person he'd been then, and, by confessing, begin to forgive himself.

Finally *So Long, See You Tomorrow* is a book about mercy from someone who understands that we all need it. Maybe, before I read it, I was unaware of that. I know it now.

STEWART O'NAN is the author of ten novels, including *Snow Angels*, *A Prayer for the Dying*, and *The Good Wife*.

The Myth of Sisyphus

Albert Camus

Jacques Pépin

When I was thirteen years of age, I left school of my own volition. My parents had a restaurant, and I wanted to immerse myself in the world of cooking, following my mother's example. If I had been asked at the time what the most important books of my life were, I probably would have said Alexandre Dumas' *The Three Musketeers* and *The Count of Monte Cristo.*

At seventeen, after an apprenticeship and a summer job cooking at the spa/resort of Aix-les-Bains, I moved on to Paris and ended up at the Plaza Athénée, where I would work from 1953 to 1959. One of the finest hotels in Paris, it had a great social program, including soccer and basketball, along with a library that was at our disposal. I must confess that I still have in my possession Dante's *Divine Comedy*, which I "borrowed" from the library at the Plaza Athénée. Another benefit of the job was that on our day off each week, we could eat at the special employees' restaurant at the hotel.

Movies were prohibitively expensive, so when we went out it was often to see live theater, which was subsidized by the government. France's national theater, the Comédie-Française, is one of the best performance companies in the world, with two theaters in Paris presenting the classics of Molière, Voltaire, Sartre, Anouilh, and others. The price to sit in the *poulailler* (the highest gallery seats, farthest from the stage) for a play or for a comic opera production of Offenbach's *La vie parisienne,* say, was no more than the price of playing a jukebox recording. It was about the only entertainment my friends and I could afford, and the superb performances prompted us to do more reading. I moved on from *The Three Musketeers* to Zola's *Nana*, Balzac's *Le cousin Pons*, Flaubert's *Madame Bovary*, and George Sand's *La petite Fadette*, shifting from the classics to trash novels, trying to educate myself, although I would not go back to formal study until I came to the United States in 1959.

In the middle of the 1950s, French existentialism was à la mode. I worked in a restaurant in Montparnasse where Sartre was a regular. He was very homely, with thick reading glasses, a pale complexion, and a receding hairline, but I was fascinated as I watched him reading intently and eating indifferently. In this after-war period of dark romanticism, blues and jazz were playing in all the clubs of Paris, and Juliette Gréco was singing somber love songs in her raspy voice. Sidney Bechet and Louis Armstrong were my heroes, nihilism and existentialism were the rage of the day, and Camus, Jaspers, and Sartre wrote about free will and existential anguish.

Camus sounded less didactic and more human to me than Sartre. He had a more hopeful aesthetic view of the world, even though, like Sartre—and unlike Jaspers—he was an atheistic existentialist. The first works of Camus' I read were *The Stranger* and a play, *The Misunderstanding*, which was being performed at the time in a Parisian theater. I was taken with *The Stranger*, intrigued by the story and fascinated with the main character, although I did not truly understand Camus' message at the time. I went on to read *The Myth of Sisyphus*, which had been published in France in 1942, the same year *The Stranger* was published, and after struggling through *Sisyphus* a couple of times, I reread *The Stranger*, with a better comprehension.

The Myth of Sisyphus is a book about the absurdity of man's condition in a world without God. In Greek mythology, Sisyphus is a mortal who dies and is granted permission by Hades, the god of the Underworld, to return to Earth for a limited time. Seduced by the beauty of Earth, he breaks his promise and refuses to return to the Underworld until a decree of the gods forces him to do so. He is blinded and condemned for the rest of eternity to push a rock to the top of a mountain, but it always rolls back down and he must begin all over. The tale of Sisyphus is a metaphor for the absurdity of life: you are born, you live, and eventually you die. At first glance, there is no sense or reason in life. For Camus, religion originates as a palliative for the absurdity of life, something that gives people hope.

Yet we are rarely conscious of our absurd condition. We go along day to day, having dinner, making plans with friends, marrying, having children, enjoying all the little things that make life happier. We go through our lives without realizing the foolishness of it all. Only occasionally the window opens and someone realizes the profound senselessness of life and, unable to cope, commits suicide. The question Camus addresses is whether or not suicide is the alternative to a senseless life.

The opening of *The Myth of Sisyphus* is lapidary prose: "There is but one truly serious philosophical problem, and that is suicide. Judging whether life is or is not worth living amounts to answering the fundamental question of philosophy." On first reading, I thought Camus was a proponent of suicide. After a few more readings, I understood his message: even with the absurdities, suicide is never an option and can never be justified.

The Charlie Chaplin movie *Modern Times*, mentioned by Camus, is another metaphor for the absurdity of life. In a comical yet somber way, Chaplin exemplifies the futility and meaninglessness of working on an assembly line and tightening a bolt over and over again. However, what Camus is saying is that there is reason to be hopeful, that man must understand his condition and must struggle, fight, and rebel against the absurdity of life. There is hope, and hope is to be found in man and in man only. Man defines himself, gives himself an identity through his actions. Even though the futility of our condition leads us all to the same end, we must and can dignify life through our deeds and behavior.

Sisyphus is the ultimate absurd hero, but Camus says that we must think of him as a "happy man." He sees Sisyphus on the way up the hill as representing the struggle against life: shoulder pressed to the rock, sweating, cursing, pushing. At that point, Sisyphus doesn't appeal to our emotional sense as much as he does at the top of the hill, just before the rock starts rolling back down. On the way down, he has the time to think and prepare himself to begin pushing the rock up the hill all over again. It is then that Sisyphus is most interesting, when he is conscious of his condition, looking at it and accepting it as a man, accepting the totality of it to show that he is stronger than the destiny imposed upon him by fate.

Reading *The Myth of Sisyphus* stimulated my mind and made me want to study and understand more. I felt comfortable with Camus' point of view. It was a catalyst for the studies I did after coming to the United States. I do not know whether authorities on the writings of Camus would agree with my evaluation of *The Myth of Sisyphus*, but for me it was a book that corresponded with my ideas of life. We must be responsible for our actions. We have to believe in man, in his power, dignity, and goodness, and in his ability to create a responsible life of his own. Camus' book taught me never to give up against the nether side of life. Sisyphus is not a fatalist; he doesn't accept his own condition but fights to the end, giving us a lesson on the value of life. We must struggle in the face of misfortune, and when age takes a toll and the end gets nearer, we must fight against sickness and decrepitude.

I think that consciously and unconsciously those points have always been with me, serving as a guiding light. To that extent, I am still under the influence of Camus, and will continue to be so until the end of my "absurd" life.

JACQUES PÉPIN's latest public television series, his ninth, debuted in the fall of 2004. It is based on his cookbook of the same title, *Jacques Pépin: Fast Food My Way.* He is the author of numerous other cookbooks as well as a bestselling memoir, *The Apprentice: My Life in the Kitchen*. A contributing editor to *Food & Wine* magazine, and one of America's best-known chefs, cooking teachers, and cookbook authors, Pépin serves as dean of special programs at the French Culinary Institute in New York City and teaches at Boston University. Before moving to the United States in 1959, he was the personal chef to three French heads of state, including Charles de Gaulle, and in 2004 he was awarded France's highest civilian honor, the French Legion of Honor. He resides in Madison, Connecticut, with his wife, Gloria.

The Man Who Was Thursday

G. K. Chesterton

Anne Perry

A good book changes you, even if it is only to add a little to the furniture of your mind. It will make you laugh and perhaps cry; it should certainly make you think. A great book will make you dream in regions you have never dared to before, and ultimately it will spur you to create or achieve something new yourself.

For me G. K. Chesterton's *The Man Who Was Thursday* is a book to light fires in my mind, uplift my heart, tell me truths I had only glimpsed before. It makes me feel wonderfully unique, and at the same time part of all mankind. If you think that is too much for one book, read it, and see if it doesn't do the same for you. Read it again a few years later, and find it does so even more powerfully.

It seems an absurd title. What sort of a book is it? Chesterton himself, in an essay written in 1936 and published the day before he died, called it "melodramatic moonshine" and pointed out that he had subtitled it *A Nightmare.* I would say it is more of a vision, in the sense of something unreal that makes reality suddenly easier to understand. Sorry! The Chesterton passion for paradox is contagious.

It is a marvelous adventure of six men with enormous courage fighting against the anarchy in the world, against those who would destroy, whether by bombs or by indifference. They battle all kinds of dangers, and are pursued from England to France and back again. Some of the chases are deeply sinister, some wild, some desperate, some hilarious, some totally bizarre. The last is the most fantastic of all. If I say it includes riding on an elephant and in a hot-air balloon, and appears to end in something close to the end of the world, or a fancy dress party in the garden of heaven, you will catch the idea.

And yet the issues are as real as bread and butter, or today's terrorism in the streets. It is a fantasy, in the best sense that it is the imagination set free. Within a fantasy's own logic of meaning, its morality, there are no boundaries as to what a writer may use to enrich the picture.

It is a poem in prose. The sunset over Saffron Park: ". . . but towards the west the whole grew past description, transparent and passionate, and the last red-hot plumes of it covered up the sun like something too good to be seen."

There is far more, a hundred passages immeasurably enriching to the memory of beauty, the vividness of life, the sheer love of the earth and the gift to savor it and be grateful. I do not see a pink tree in blossom without thinking of the one before which Gabriel Syme fell on his knees when he expected to die. The music of words, the color and depth, are there all the way through. Chesterton was a poet, he could scarcely help it.

But he was also a thinker, a believer, a man who dared to dream. *The Man Who Was Thursday* is above all a journey of the spirit where men love the good in the world enough to fight for it. Even though each believes himself utterly alone, and that the enemy is too many, too strong for him ever to win, he cannot turn away or betray the light he has once seen. One short quotation from the end summarizes the heart of it.

> "But you were men. You did not forget your secret honour, though the whole cosmos turned an engine of torture to tear it out of you. I knew how near you were to hell. I know how

you, Thursday, crossed swords with King Satan, and how you, Wednesday, named me in the hour without hope."

The Man Who Was Thursday is vast and wise, filled with words and ideas that make sense of pain and loneliness and the length of the whole journey of life. But you need to read it for yourself, perhaps many times.

How has it changed me? It tells me that I am only walking the same path as all mankind, and not only that it makes sense but it is the only way that possibly could do. I may imagine I am alone, and that is necessary too, but I am not, I am simply in my own part of the procession.

Chesterton's great book gives me food, armor, and a compass for the soul. It tells me yet again that the power of the word is like the power of light itself. I will read, and I will also write! I will write something that will be food, light, and armor for others.

Thank you, Chesterton, for the passion of your mind. You died before I was born, but I like to think you would have approved at least some of the things I have done, and will yet do.

Anne Perry is the widely acclaimed author of two best-selling mystery series set in Victorian London: the Charlotte and Thomas Pitt novels, including *Seven Dials* and *Long Spoon Lane*, and the William Monk novels, most recently *Dark Assassin*. She has also written three novels set during World War I, *No Graves As Yet*, *Shoulder the Sky*, and *Angels in the Gloom*. A recipient of the Edgar Award and the Herodotus Lifetime Achievement Award for Excellence in Historical Mysteries, she lives in Scotland. You can visit her at www.anneperry.net.

A Child's Garden of Verses

ROBERT LOUIS STEVENSON

and more

JACK PRELUTSKY

This is a challenge! My parents taught me to read before I went to kindergarten, and I started reading books not long after I learned to walk, so it's hard to pick just one book. Instead I'd like to tell you about a number of books that greatly affected me in different stages of my life.

The first book I remember reading on my own was *A Child's Garden of Verses*, by Robert Louis Stevenson. How I loved those delightful little poems with their charming illustrations—I still go back and read them from time to time. That may have been the book that first sparked my love of poetry.

Later I read *Alice in Wonderland* and *Through the Looking Glass*, by Lewis Carroll, and was enchanted by the magical worlds he created. Not counting nursery rhymes, the first poem I ever memorized was "Jabberwocky," from *Through the Looking Glass.* I still know it, and enjoy reciting it aloud every once in a while.

When I was in junior high, now mostly called middle school, I fell in love with *Wild Animals I Have Known*, by Ernest Thompson Seton. I hid the book in an obscure place in the school library so it was always waiting for me, and read it a couple of dozen times. I was captivated by the stories of a wolf named Lobo, a cottontail rabbit called Raggylug, and Silverspot the crow. Seton's book helped instill a deep love of nature in me, and it certainly influenced my own writing. In fact, his book is probably a major reason why my first books of poetry were about animals.

I've surely been affected by many other books, but those I've mentioned here remain deep inside me. I still have copies of all of them in my home.

One of the best-loved children's poets of our time, JACK PRELUTSKY is the author of more than forty books of verse for children, including *The New Kid on the Block, Something Big Has Been Here, The Dragons Are Singing Tonight, A Pizza the Size of the Sun, It's Raining Pigs and Noodles, Scranimals, If Not for the Cat*, and *Nightmares: Poems to Trouble Your Sleep.* He has also edited many acclaimed collections, among them *The 20th Century Children's Poetry Treasury, The Random House Book of Poetry for Children*, and *The Beauty of the Beast: Poems from the Animal Kingdom*. He lives in Washington State with his wife, Carolynn.

A Clockwork Orange

ANTHONY BURGESS

IAN RANKIN

I grew up in a small coal-mining town on the east coast of Scotland. Soon after I was born, the coal started running out, and a little bit of hope trickled away from my birthplace. I had a pretty active imagination. I'd pretend my terraced house was a spaceship with me at the controls. I'd read a lot of comics, then try making my own, even though I was useless at drawing. When I was eleven or twelve, I started listening to pop music and formed a band . . . but only in my head and on paper. The band was called the Amoebas, and I would write their lyrics, plan their world tours, design their album sleeves. From those doggerel lyrics, poems started to emerge—not that this was something I could tell anyone about. The kids I hung around with would have given me a slap. My parents were supportive, but not great readers. Both of them had left school young, seen the war through, and ended up as manual workers. They weren't professional people or well educated. I was the first person in my family to make it to senior high school (that is, I stayed on to eighteen rather than leaving at sixteen). In time, I'd also be the first member of my family to attend university. So I sat quietly in my bedroom and scribbled my thoughts and ideas down on paper, keeping it all hidden from those around me.

Then *A Clockwork Orange* came along. I was aware of the film first, mostly because of the controversy it caused. Teenagers would dress in the same clothing as the droogs and try to wreak havoc. As a result, director Stanley Kubrick pulled the film from the United Kingdom, giving me no prospect of seeing it. But then a mate at school loaned me his older brother's copy of the book, opening up a whole new world. I discovered that there was no "rating" on books—anybody could read anything. I was too young to see *The Godfather*, but the local library gladly loaned me Mario Puzo's book. I began to see literature as this wonderfully illicit and transgressive form, and I wanted more of it. But *A Clockwork Orange* was my favorite. For one thing, its author, Anthony Burgess, was a man in love with language, and that passion transmitted itself to me. For another, he seemed to be talking about kids like me, dead-enders stuck in tedious towns, who hung around the streets and occasionally got into large-scale fights with rival gangs. This meant I could extrapolate from my own life—I didn't have to write about pop stars or spaceships. I started to write poems and short stories about my hometown and the people I knew there. By the age of sixteen, I'd written a short novel about high school, and had won second prize in a national poetry competition. I was on my way to becoming a writer, thanks to Anthony Burgess and *A Clockwork Orange.*

IAN RANKIN is the author of the Inspector Rebus novels, which have won literary awards in the United States, the United Kingdom, Germany, France, Italy, Denmark, and Finland. Six of his books have been televised. He was awarded the Order of the British Empire by Her Majesty Queen Elizabeth II, and his work has been translated into twenty-seven languages. He lives in Edinburgh.

Out of My Life and Thought

ALBERT SCHWEITZER

The Doctor Dolittle Series

HUGH LOFTING

RICHARD RHODES

Lost in the middle of adolescence; a ward of the Jackson County Juvenile Court living at a private boys' home, a farm outside Independence, Missouri; my father lost to me when his wife, the stepmother of my former torment, was barred from the premises and kept him away; looking for an anchor, a source of meaning in the world; I came across Albert Schweitzer. He'd been looking for meaning too, he wrote in his autobiography, *Out of My Life and Thought*.

He was German, a scholar and a concert organist, but then, feeling unfulfilled, went back to school, became a physician, assembled a boatload of medical supplies, and shipped out to the Belgian Congo as a missionary. Even in Africa, starting a hospital and tending the sick, he was still tormented by the dilemma of discovering some ethical basis for civilization, an elemental anchorage that might make ethics more real.

He found it riding up the Congo on an old riverboat, steaming through a herd of hippopotamuses flashing in the afternoon light. "Reverence for Life," he called his vision. "A man is ethical," he explained to me, "only when life, as such, is sacred to him, that of plants and animals as well as that of his fellowman, and when he devotes himself helpfully to all life that is in need of help."

Well, who knows now, half a century later, what I thought that meant then. I'd grown up catch-as-catch-can in the 1940s in the streets of Kansas City, eating out of dumpsters; I was living and working on a farm. The book was an entrance into alien worlds: German philosophy, theological scholarship (*The Quest of the Historical Jesus* was Schweitzer's most radical work), the history of organ building, Africa. If you lose your parents, you cobble your life together as best you can. Better *Out of My Life and Thought* than, say, *The Fountainhead*.

What I realized only many years later was that I had been tuned to Schweitzer—multilingual, a physician living and working in Africa, running a bush hospital, professing reverence for all life including the animals—during childhood years when I devoured, one after another and then around again, Hugh Lofting's tales of Doctor Dolittle and his sturdy boy sidekick, Tommy Stubbins, c'est moi.

I didn't become a missionary, as I had thought I might. I did read German philosophy (and French and English and American), visit Africa and write about it, try to write helpfully about all life that is in need of help. Twenty-one books later, I continue to admire Schweitzer's ethical resolution—those flashing hippos breaking through all that Germanic reserve. But Doctor Dolittle and Tommy Stubbins dining with Dab-Dab and Chee-Chee, playing Blind Travel, in their excitement waking up Miranda the Bird-of-Paradise, preparing to sail off to Spidermonkey Island, the very island where Long Arrow was last seen on earth—I'm still trying to tell a story that well.

RICHARD RHODES is the author of twenty-one books, including *The Making of the Atomic Bomb*, which won a Pulitzer

Prize in General Nonfiction, a National Book Award, and a National Book Critics Circle Award; *Dark Sun: The Making of the Hydrogen Bomb*, which was short-listed for a Pulitzer Prize in History; a biography, *John James Audubon: The Making of an American*; and a memoir of childhood, *A Hole in the World*. A recipient of numerous fellowships for research and writing, including grants from the Guggenheim Foundation and the Alfred P. Sloan Foundation, he has been a visiting scholar at Harvard, MIT, and Stanford, and a host and correspondent for documentaries on American public television. He lectures frequently to audiences in the United States and abroad. He and his wife, Ginger Rhodes, a clinical psychologist in private practice, live in northern California.

Act One

Moss Hart

Frank Rich

The timing couldn't have been better when Moss Hart's autobiography, *Act One*, arrived by mail in 1959 as my mother's selection from the Book-of-the-Month Club. I was ten years old, hopelessly infatuated with Broadway, and marooned in the sleepy southern town of Washington, D.C. I didn't quite know who Moss Hart was, but his name was familiar from the record jacket of *My Fair Lady*, the hit musical he had directed, which I longed to run away and see, along with every other show in New York. Mom, an elementary school teacher, instinctually knew that *Act One* would lure me into the world of "grown-up" books, and so it did.

Act One is still my favorite American autobiography, and I do mean American. It's a Horatio Alger story about a poor boy from the Bronx who fights his way to success against overwhelming odds and lives (we are led to believe) happily ever after. But that's the plot of almost every American autobiography. *Act One* changed my life because its particular variation on the theme hit so close to home.

When the book opens, young Moss is twelve and consumed by "dreams of glory . . . quite unlike those of the other boys on the block." So was I. Though his dreams, like mine, were all about Broadway, he had yet to see Broadway. Neither had I. And though he imagined that his parents loved him, he learned early on that love can have its limits. His childhood, like mine, was roiled by violent familial storms that he, like me, didn't yet have the wisdom to understand.

Before *Act One*, I had never encountered a story that so matched my own in all its yearning, confusion, and fear. By articulating the thoughts and feelings I could not, Moss Hart made me realize that I wasn't nearly as alone as I had believed. He also made me laugh. Somehow he found uproarious humor, even farce, in the setbacks he refused to let defeat him.

More important still, *Act One* showed me a way out of my childhood. If Moss Hart could escape his circumstances through hard work, luck, the kindness of strangers, and the sheer force of his passion, maybe I could too. To this day, I find few scenes as powerful as that climactic moment when Moss, in his jubilant first flush of success, liberates his family from their impoverished digs, then throws open a window to let rain pour in and drown their unhappy past.

Of course the past is not so easily obliterated. When I reread *Act One* as an adult, I'm always struck by the shadows, silences, and evasions I didn't notice when I first read it as a child; I no longer see just the young Moss I first met some forty-five years ago, I see the book's author too, the middle-aged Moss who is looking back at his youth. I've outgrown many things since I first read *Act One*, but I can't imagine ever outgrowing *Act One*.

FRANK RICH, a columnist at *The New York Times*, was the paper's chief theater critic from 1980 to 1993 and is the author of *Ghost Light: A Memoir*.

I Know Why the Caged Bird Sings

MAYA ANGELOU

SARK

I lived in two places the summer of my sixteenth year. I'd built a small perch in the apple tree branches in my backyard, and kept my favorite books there on a tiny crooked shelf. The other place where I truly lived and breathed was the public library. I had decided to read every book in alphabetical order, shelf by shelf, and found myself captivated by what was on the *A* shelf. The library was also where I went to build a world other than the one I was living in with my family, which was a world of incest and physical abuse.

When I first saw the title *I Know Why the Caged Bird Sings*, by Maya Angelou, I instantly felt I was that bird in the cage, peering sadly out. This book's pages dissolved the bars of my cage, and I felt myself fly free for the first time. Maya Angelou's story came roaring into my life at a time when I couldn't find anything substantial written about someone who was molested or abused and was okay afterward. Maya was not only okay, she was fully herself, and telling all about her life in vivid detail—especially the parts that people usually kept secret.

I went to hear Maya Angelou speak at the same library where I'd found her book, and clearly saw her invincible spirit as she talked to the group. Right there, sitting on that folding chair, I decided to have no more shame about the abuse that had happened to me. As she signed my copy of the book, I told her this, and she reached out and held my hands with so much love it purely melted me.

I Know Why the Caged Bird Sings instilled in me the pivotal message that I could transcend the nightmare of incest and abuse. Many years later, when I finally wrote my books and told my own true-life stories, Maya Angelou was right there to write endorsements for my work and cheer me on. We appeared on a national television show together to discuss how she had mentored me through her writing, and how I in turn had mentored others through mine. Her words helped me become a phenomenal woman myself, and lift up other souls. My own soul now flies free, and I'm so grateful that I can return the gifts that were given to me through that remarkable book I found in the *A* section in a Minneapolis, Minnesota, public library.

SARK (Susan Ariel Rainbow Kennedy) is the bestselling author and artist of thirteen books, including *Succulent Wild Woman*, *Make Your Creative Dreams REAL*, and *SARK's New Creative Companion*. She is also the founder of Planet SARK, a company that develops products and services to inspire people to think and live more creatively. An acclaimed speaker and teacher, she is featured in the PBS series *Women of Wisdom and Power.* You can visit her at www.planetsark.com.

Angela's Ashes

FRANK McCOURT

LISA SCOTTOLINE

Every book I read changes me in some way, which is the very reason I read, and why books matter. But not every book has changed my life; not every book has that power, nor every author that skill. In recent memory, I can think of only one book that meets the test. For me, it's *Angela's Ashes,* by Frank McCourt.

Let me tell you something about why I picked up *Angela's Ashes* in the first place, well before it had achieved the praise it would later, and so deservedly, gather. I bought *Angela's Ashes* because I liked the cover. It showed a photograph of a small boy with a sideways smile and a little jacket and adorably dirty toes. I assumed the cover photo was of the author as a child, which I later learned, with a vague sense of disillusionment, was incorrect. But by that time, I'd fallen in love with Frank McCourt. I still love him, though we've never met. That's another reason books matter; they connect people, soul to soul.

If the cover of *Angela's Ashes* made me pick it up, the description on its inside flap almost made me put it down. The copy said that *Angela's Ashes* was a memoir of the author's impoverished childhood. At that, I admit I had a politically incorrect thought: please, God, deliver me from another impoverished-childhood memoir. I would have set the book back on the shelf, but somehow I couldn't leave the little boy with the dirty toes. I bought the book and read it on the plane home.

I couldn't put it down. I was as engrossed as if it had been a page-turner. I laughed out loud. I cried into my United Airlines napkin. I lived and loved every single word of Frank McCourt's impoverished childhood. I actually gasped when I read the last line, because it is the best-written last line in any book, anywhere.

Angela's Ashes reminded me of the single most important element in a book, be it fiction or nonfiction, and that is the power of voice. Loosely defined, voice is the way the story is told. For example, around your dinner table, your mother tells a story differently from the way your teenager does. Each has a unique voice. Not all writers have a voice, but Frank McCourt has voice to burn, and voice enough to render subject matter beside the point. By that I mean, you may think you've heard stories about impoverished childhoods before, just as I did, but you've never heard Frank McCourt's story, as told by him, until you have read *Angela's Ashes.*

Which is when you realize that *Angela's Ashes* is about much more than Frank McCourt's own childhood. Because it's so beautifully realized and rendered that it actually becomes about everything, all at once. (I'm not drunk, I swear.) It's about the immigrant experience; it's about the human experience. It's about being so poor that you die. It's about being so hungry that scrambled eggs bring you to tears. It's about survival and triumph. It's about the promise of this country, fulfilled. It's about a mother's love, and more touchingly, a child's.

This is not the kind of stuff you can put on a book flap, or people will think you're drunk, but the truth is:

Angela's Ashes will break your heart and put it back together again, but better.

LISA SCOTTOLINE is a *New York Times* bestselling author of thirteen suspense novels, most recently *Dirty Blonde.* Born and raised in Philadelphia, she earned a degree in English from the

University of Pennsylvania in just three years and went on to graduate cum laude from the university's law school, where she is currently teaching a course called Justice and Fiction. All of her books draw on her experience as a trial lawyer and her clerkships in the state and federal judicial systems. She is a mother, a die-hard Eagles fan, and a winner of the Edgar Award and *Cosmopolitan*'s Fun Fearless Female Award, among many other honors.

The Human Comedy

WILLIAM SAROYAN

BERNIE S. SIEGEL, M.D.

I must begin by saying I do not believe any book can change your life; only you can. Two people read the same book, one is inspired while the other is bored. The issue is not the book but the person—what lies within each of us. The author's wisdom combined with the reader's inspiration and desire to change can lead to a new life for the reader.

The book that has meant the most to me in my life is *The Human Comedy*, by William Saroyan. When I was struggling with many issues, particularly loss, as a physician caring for and counseling people with life-threatening illnesses, I came across a story by Saroyan called "The Daring Young Man on the Flying Trapeze." At the end of the story the young man dies after thinking about a trapeze to God, and becomes "dreamless, unalive, perfect." From then on I sought out all of Saroyan's books.

For me life is a tragic comedy. In *The Human Comedy*, Saroyan deals with loss. When the novel opens, Mr. Macauley has died and his son Marcus has gone off to war and is later killed. How does a family survive all this pain?

I see the pain of most people's lives, and particularly their childhoods. I see the pain of those who grew up being told they were failures, no good at anything, and were dressed only in dark colors. So many grow up feeling unloved and hearing destructive messages from their parents that lead to their not caring for themselves. In *The Human Comedy*, Saroyan has a teacher talk to one of her students and tell him what we all need to hear to survive: to respect each other even if we don't like each other; to love truth and honor; not to be alike but to be human in our own way and to pay no attention to those trying to hold us back and embarrass us. These are precepts we need to hear from our parents, precepts we need to live by.

Perhaps the most important words in Saroyan's book for me were these: "But try to remember that a good man can never die. . . . The person of a man may leave—or be taken away—but the best part of a good man stays. It stays forever. Love is immortal and makes all things immortal. But hate dies every minute." Those words, and the thought that when we leave our bodies we become perfect again, have sustained me through much loss. From my experience, I believe they speak the truth.

Saroyan writes from wisdom. He knows what I learned: "Doctors don't know everything. . . . They understand matter, not spirit." Medical education is not a true education. It is more about information and matter, and not about spirit and the real world people exist in. Saroyan has Mrs. Macauley tell one of her sons that nothing good ever ends and that all things are part of us and we must thank God for them. He fills *The Human Comedy* with meaningful messages. The evil man must be forgiven and loved because something of us is in him and something of him is in us. We must give of everything we have, for if we give to a thief he cannot steal from us, and then he is no longer a thief, and the more we give the more we will have to give. We must not fear all the wonderful mistakes we must and will make. No matter what the mistakes are, we must not be afraid of having made them or of making more of them.

If every child were brought up with the words spoken in *The Human Comedy*, the world would be a very different place.

Last but not least, there is a scene in the novel where little Ulysses Macauley sees a penny and his brother Homer tells him,

"Pick it up, Ulysses, it's good luck. Keep it—always." I have always believed that finding pennies is a sign from God that I am on the right path. I spoke to Saroyan's daughter once, and she told me her father was like that and would run out into traffic to pick up a penny he'd spotted. The ultimate sign for me was finding twenty-six cents when I was about to run a marathon, which is twenty-six miles long. It was a sure sign I was going to make it.

Why? Because the penny says it all: In God We Trust, and we have the liberty to be the unique and authentic person we want to be and not what others impose, and there's Abe Lincoln, staring into the east where the sun rises, so he cannot see any shadows, but still without a smile. Would he have lived differently if he knew what was coming in his life?

I have learned to accept my mortality, and I will love until I am tired of my body. Then I will leave and become perfect and immortal.

BERNIE S. SIEGEL, M.D., is the author of *Love, Medicine and Miracles* and many other groundbreaking books on the healing powers of the human mind and will, including *How to Live Between Office Visits*, *Prescriptions for Living*, and *101 Exercises for the Soul*. In 1978 he originated Exceptional Cancer Patients, a form of therapy utilizing patients' drawings, dreams, images, and feelings. ECaP is based on "carefrontation," a safe, loving therapeutic confrontation that facilitates personal empowerment and healing. As a physician, Bernie embraces a philosophy of living and dying that stands at the forefront of the medical and spiritual issues our society grapples with today. He and his wife, Bobbie, live in a suburb of New Haven, Connecticut, where they have coauthored books, articles, and five children.

Kitty Foyle

CHRISTOPHER MORLEY

Voltaire! Voltaire!

GUY ENDORE

LIZ SMITH

There wasn't much of my life to change at age sixteen when I read Christopher Morley's *Kitty Foyle.* I was so green behind the ears that I was ripe for anything. But after reading and rereading Mr. Morley's first-person story where, incredibly, he submerged himself into his Philadelphia heroine, the feisty and Irish Kitty, I was a goner. I wanted to be like Kitty—smart, independent, ambitious. And I wanted to leave home (Texas) and go to New York just as Kitty did, where she became a whiz in the ad business. *Kitty Foyle* taught me for the first time that women need to be independent and in charge of their own lives no matter how much they moon around about Mr. Right. I mooned around anyway, but I did get off my duff and into college and direct to the Big City. Kitty was my inspiration.

My other revelation came to me when I read Guy Endore's *Voltaire! Voltaire!* I began to reexamine the religious background in which I'd been raised. I fell in love with an outrageously brilliant Frenchman and I began to question and seek. I guess now I'm just a deathbed Christian like Voltaire. Guy Endore's book had a profound effect on me at a time when my intellect at the very least needed stretching.

LIZ SMITH is the author of *The Mother Book*, *Natural Blonde*, and *Dishing*. She is currently at work on *Sex After Death: Heaven Goes Hollywood*.

The Red and the Black

STENDHAL

EDWARD SOREL

As an art student at Cooper Union in 1949, I was required to take an art survey class taught by Paul Zuckerman. Zuckerman was a German Jew who spoke with an accent. Like many Jews, he was extremely erudite. Like many Germans, he held nutty theories about genetics. Somewhere between the Renaissance and Impressionism he suddenly veered off art to tell us about the theories of Ernst Kretschmer, a German psychiatrist who believed that one's body type determined one's personality. There were three types: pyknic (fat), athletic (muscular), and aesthenic (thin).

Zuckerman explained what sort of personality traits each body type produced, but assured us that most people are mixtures of all three. He selected three boys and three girls as examples. I was chosen as the perfect aesthenic, and, along with the others, had to stand in front of the class. "Notice ze long vingers und narrow jest cavity," Zuckerman said when he came to me. He then expanded into figures from literature and movies. For the aesthenic type he picked Fred Astaire (hey, I thought, maybe this isn't so bad after all), and from fiction, Julien Sorel, the hero of *The Red and the Black*, a novel by someone named Stendhal. I had never heard of him.

Naturally, I read the book. Although it takes place in France under the Bourbon restoration, it was easy for me to empathize with Julien Sorel. Like me, Julien hated his father, distrusted all authority, and thought religion was for the mentally handicapped. He was also tall, thin, handsome, sensitive, and very bright. His apparent resemblance to me was uncanny, except that he didn't wear glasses and he was catnip to women. Every beautiful woman Julian met went to bed with him.

Some years later, when I decided I no longer wished to have the same surname as my father—Schwartz—I had no problem choosing an alternative.

EDWARD SOREL's latest book, *Literary Lives*, was published this spring by Bloomsbury Books. He is a frequent contributor to *The New Yorker* and *Vanity Fair.*

The End of the Road

JOHN BARTH

JANE STERN

In the summer of 1964 I went with my family to a peaceful cabin on the shores of Lake Winnipesaukee in New Hampshire. Among the relatives was my uncle Henry, whom I adored. He was a psychoanalyst who taught at Yale and looked like an Ivy League Clark Gable.

Henry made it his business to bring me his current favorite book to read, and then we'd discuss it as we floated together in the middle of the lake in a canoe. That summer the book was John Barth's *The End of the Road*, nihilistic and depressing. Just the kind of book that would make anyone want to jump out of a canoe in the middle of a lake and drown.

I was an alienated seventeen-year-old, so what could be better than to sit with my uncle the shrink far from the happy crowds on shore and discuss Barth's depiction of a gruesome botched abortion and his sense of overwhelming angst? Not until I was in my forties did I realize that just about every book given to me by my book-loving family was morbid and existentially bleak. *The End of the Road* was perfect for a girl who had cut her literary teeth on *The Lonely Doll* and classic animal stories about brave dogs who get killed or maimed.

It took me years of psychoanalysis to deprogram myself from the family despair. But as an EMT with the Georgetown Fire Department, I have to admit that when a 911 call goes out for a "crisis intervention" (a suicide attempt or other psychiatric emergency) I am always first on scene.

JANE STERN is the author of the widely praised memoir *Ambulance Girl: How I Saved Myself by Becoming an EMT.* With her husband, Michael, she has written more than thirty books chronicling the millions of miles they've logged and the countless meals they've eaten in their quest for the best of American food, from chili to banana splits, from pulled pork to pound cake. She is also a contributing editor and columnist at *Gourmet* magazine, a regular contributor to National Public Radio's *The Splendid Table*, and a winner of the James Beard Award for Lifetime Achievement. She and Michael live in West Redding, Connecticut.

The Sears Catalogue

Michael Stern

I was an insatiable reader as a child, devouring every book I found about adventurous men and intrepid animals in jungles, outer space, and the Old West. The one I liked best, and still read every couple of years, was Will James' magical equine biography, *Smoky the Cow Horse*; but the one that changed my life, and the one I used to read the most, was the Sears catalogue.

It was my window on the world. Poring over the Sears catalogue and looking at its pictures taught me more about everything than anything I have ever read. I relished reading about the materiel of lives that were nothing like my own. Where else could a nice Jewish boy growing up in a polite Midwestern suburb learn the differences between gas-powered and electric-powered arc welders, the advantage of a short-throw, lever-action hunting rifle, the serenity to be found in a family Bible with self-pronouncing type, and the superiority of let-out skins over split skins in a mink stole? The pages devoted to ladies' panties, industrial-strength girdles, and brassieres, I confess, were my first thrilling exposure to cheesecake dreams of the female form.

Like modern niche catalogues devoted to a specific lifestyle or demographic, Sears' all-inclusive illustrations and descriptions were not about reality but rather a flawless vision of it in which clothes fit well, tools do their job, and everybody can find exactly what they need, whatever that may be. In this one comprehensive volume is twentieth-century America's ideal image of itself.

MICHAEL STERN is the coauthor, with his wife, Jane, of more than thirty books about popular culture, including the bestsellers *Elvis World* and *The Encyclopedia of Bad Taste*, the culinary classics *Roadfood* and *Square Meals*, and the recently published memoir *Two for the Road*. Michael studied art history at the University of Michigan and Yale and received a master's degree in film history from Columbia University. The Sterns' current work includes the James Beard Award–winning column "Roadfood" in *Gourmet*, weekly segments on National Public Radio's *The Splendid Table*, and the Web site Roadfood.com.

Letters to a Young Poet

RAINER MARIA RILKE

ALEXANDRA STODDARD

When I was struggling to write my first book in 1966, a senior editor at *Reader's Digest*, Robert O'Brien, a writer, came to me one day with a stretcher from grace to save me: he told me to read *Letters to a Young Poet*, by Rainer Maria Rilke.

This one book is indispensable to me, and has been for forty years. In ten letters written from 1903 to 1908, Rilke answers yearning questions from a young poet, Franz Xaver Kappus. Rilke's classic book bestows invaluable insight, advice, and confidence on those of us trying to find meaning and purpose in our complex lives.

The wisdom Rilke passes on to young Mr. Kappus covers a deep and wide range of high principles.

- Be patient with ourselves and others.
- Practice humility.
- Trust our intuition.
- Be personally responsible for our inward discipline.
- Learn about ourselves through solitude.
- Concentrate through contemplation of life from our highest perspective.
- Appreciate the beauty and good in nature and all things.
- Live the poetic spirit every day.

Rilke was an admirer of the powerful sculptor Auguste Rodin. He not only studied Rodin's life and works but also wrote enthusiastically about him. Eventually they lived in a little stone house together, where Rilke acted as a sort of secretary. He felt Rodin lived in his art and everything in his life grew toward that art—and only that. Rodin taught Rilke tenacious persistence, the persevering that helped him grip his own purpose. Of greatest value to Rilke was Rodin's daily example of unflagging patience.

Rilke learned to trust his own feelings, his longing to do something good. He teaches us to be patient as beginners in our necessary pursuit of some kind of excellence. He awakens us to the seriousness of living deeply, working steadily, feeling joy in our labor and self-expression, and being patient—the four cornerstones of a creative life. "Almost everything serious is difficult, and everything is serious." Do you think Scott Peck read Rilke's letters? *The Road Less Traveled* begins, "Life is difficult."

Rilke teaches us that we must find the center of our lives in our work. Our teacher read enormously and displayed tremendous inner discipline, urging the same from us. He discovered he was happiest when he was working, producing; not having written, but the actual writing, the creating, was all-important.

In these ten letters we are told to avoid seeking approval or praise—from anyone, anywhere, anytime. We come to discover that everyday life is our best subject. We begin to believe and know that quotidian life is the greatest good. We grow to understand that our most valuable wealth is a vivid, sensitive vocabulary that enables us to communicate well with ourselves and others. Rilke asserts that most events are inexpressible, that our existence is profoundly mysterious. He urges us to go into ourselves, to test the depths of our being. He urges us to make a commitment to what we choose to do, how we choose to live, what we choose to create.

> You ask whether your verses are good. . . . I beg you to give up all that. You are looking outward, and that above all you should

not do now. Nobody can counsel and help you, nobody. There is only one single way. Go into yourself. Search for the reason that bids you write; find out whether it is spreading out its roots in the deepest places of your heart. . . . seek those [themes] which your own everyday life offers you; describe your sorrows and desires, passing thoughts and the belief in some sort of beauty—describe all these with loving, quiet, humble sincerity, and use, to express yourself, the things in your environment, the images from your dreams, and the objects of your memory. If your daily life seems poor, do not blame it; blame yourself, tell yourself that you are not poet enough to call forth its riches; for to the creator there is no poverty and no poor indifferent place.

Rilke urges us to recognize that life is challenging and serious, that it is always here, in the heart of our experience of the now, that we find happiness, that we truly live the poetic spirit. These are his words: ". . . after all I do only want to advise you to keep growing quietly and seriously throughout your whole development."

Letters to a Young Poet is as fresh and inspiring today as it was nearly one hundred years ago. This master calls us to be personally responsible for the choices we make, the discipline we exhibit, the joy we find as a result.

ALEXANDRA STODDARD is the author of twenty-five books and a sought-after speaker on the art of living. Widely recognized as a pioneer of the happiness movement, she has inspired millions to pursue more fulfilling and happier lives.

The Horatio Hornblower Series

C. S. Forester

I Meet Horatio, and the Consequences

Paco Underhill

I grew up in a diplomatic family that was given home leave every two years. The summer of 1961 we were stateside visiting my grandparents in between moving from Warsaw, Poland, to Kuala Lumpur, Malaya. At that point in my life, reading, while not a chore, was not a passion either—until I met Horatio.

My grandfather loved to read to his grandchildren. While Mom read to us at bedtime, Pop, as we called him, liked to read to us outdoors, where he could smoke his pipe. He was responsible for introducing me to C. S. Forester. The book was *Mr. Midshipman Hornblower*, the first in the series of eleven books that remain in print today as the gold standard of maritime fiction. Set during the Napoleonic Wars, they trace the career of Horatio Hornblower, a British naval officer. Horatio is painfully shy, terribly self-conscious, and devastatingly class-challenged—all afflictions I still identify with.

While many men of my grandfather's generation went off to fight in France in 1917 and came back seared by the experience, for Pop, as a signal corps officer, it was the highlight of his life. Running around France laying telephone cable and drinking and eating in country cafés was the embodiment of gallantry and adventure. I am not sure if he ever fired his pistol or heard a machine gun. *Beau Geste* was his favorite movie, he spoke horribly accented French, and he had a lifelong taste for cream-based sauces. He was a good reader.

On that summer afternoon, for the first time in my life, I felt like ripping that book from my grandfather's hands because he wasn't feeding it to me fast enough. It was the magic moment when reading became escape and recreation. And although Horatio, as Forester introduces us to him, was older than my ten years, he served as a mentoring figure from whom I drew courage.

We moved on to Kuala Lumpur, where I went to a British army school that ran from eight in the morning until noon, six days a week. For the rest of the day we were flung to the corners of the city in buses equipped with Gurkha guards. I was a fat, lonely kid until I discovered that the two English-language libraries downtown had the entire Horatio Hornblower series and more books by C. S. Forester.

On my heavy Chinese-made bicycle, through tropical heat and monsoon rain, I made the pilgrimage from our suburban home into downtown Kuala Lumpur, returning one load of books and picking up another. It didn't take long for me to lose the baby fat; loneliness is something I carry to this day. The freedom to ride my bike to the library became a seminal part of my growing independence.

A year into commuting, I locked my bike and was walking at the edge of a park by the Klang River. The eating carts gave off the mixed smells of pungent Indian curries and Malay blachan fish paste. The small, dense crowd intensified those smells in sweat and proximity. I pushed my way into the center of the crowd, where, as if in a cock ring, stood two protagonists. On the left was a huge Sikh policeman, trimmed black beard under his tan uniform turban, his arms and upper legs covered in hair, puttee leggings running up his calves from black shoes. At the end of a cord anchored on his belt was the gigantic pistol he held in his right hand. I did not notice the other man until I heard the pistol fire and saw the policeman's bullet smack into his body, leaving a hole on one side the size of a quarter, and a hole on the other side the size of a fist. Like a loose dying garden hose, the man's body, as it fell, sprayed blood everywhere within the eight-foot radius where I stood.

As I withdrew to the edge of the crowd, I was horrified not by what I'd witnessed but by the darkening bloodstains on the white shirt of my school uniform. What would Horatio do? I burned my shirt before I got home, destroying the evidence. My mother would see nothing. Nothing was going to stand between me and my access to books. What I saw along the way was my business.

PACO UNDERHILL is founder, CEO, and president of Envirosell, a New York–based research and consulting firm with offices around the world. He has spent more than twenty-five years conducting research on various aspects of shopping behavior, and is a leading expert in the field. A regular contributor to NPR and BBC Radio, he has been profiled in *The New Yorker*, *Fortune*, and *BusinessWeek*, among other publications. His columns and editorials have appeared in *The New York Times*, *The Wall Street Journal*, and *The Christian Science Monitor.* He is the author of the international bestseller *Why We Buy: The Science of Shopping*, and most recently of *Call of the Mall: The Geography of Shopping.*

To Kill a Mockingbird

HARPER LEE

"HEY, BOO"

SUSAN VREELAND

Harper Lee's classic and timeless plea for tolerance, *To Kill a Mockingbird*, gives us hope that communities racked by ignorance and pretension can experience moments of grace. In a tenderly rendered Southern town in the 1930s, the lovable characters I want to throw my arms around, the honorable ones I want to emulate, and the despicable ones I want to thrash all come alive and reveal aspects of America not to be forgotten. The lessons here are not just for children.

It's a sin to kill a bird that injures no one but sends its song out for everyone to enjoy, while it's not a sin to shoot a rabid dog to alleviate its own suffering and stop the threat it poses. It's a sin to torment the different, the reclusive, the ill equipped. It's not a sin to honor an old woman struggling to free herself from a drug so she can die "beholden to nothing and nobody." It's a sin to go along with a crowd unthinkingly and succumb to hysteria and bigotry. It's not a sin to stand up for justice even if you stand alone.

These are some of the ethical principles that Atticus Finch, widower, lawyer, laconic sage, tries to teach his daughter, Jean Louise (Scout), and his son, Jem, during the crisis of conscience that rips the veil of innocence from childhood. Having undertaken to defend an innocent black man unjustly accused of raping a white woman, Atticus fails to penetrate the prejudice and the man is condemned. When the disappointed black community rises in the courtroom gallery to honor Atticus for his efforts and his values, Reverend Sykes nudges Scout, saying, "Miss Jean Louise, stand up. Your father's passin'." It's a transcendent moment.

Developing along with the story of the trial is the children's curiosity about the recluse Arthur Radley, whom they call Boo. Atticus's lessons of respect for all people and his efforts to instill in Scout a sensitive awareness of others culminate when she greets Arthur Radley with the simplicity of "Hey, Boo." It's one of the greatest lines in literature because it acknowledges a human being naturally, on his own terms, without requiring anything of him in return, which is the highest kind of love. In her tenderness toward this man who is drawn by his brave and unrequited love into the one place he feared, the public limelight, Scout Finch shows she has learned from his example the importance of caring in a profound and appropriate manner for those different from ourselves. To my way of thinking, this little girl shows us the redemptive grace of which we all are capable.

SUSAN VREELAND is the bestselling author of numerous works of historical fiction on art-related themes. Her books include *Life Studies*, a collection of stories revolving around well-known Impressionist and Postimpressionist painters; *Girl in Hyacinth Blue*, which traces an alleged Vermeer painting through the centuries; *The Passion of Artemisia*, which illuminates the inner life of Italian Baroque painter Artemisia Gentileschi; and *The Forest Lover*, which follows rebel Canadian painter Emily Carr into the wilderness of British Columbia. Vreeland's novels have been translated into twenty-five languages.

Charlotte's Web

E. B. White

Kate Walbert

The book that changed my life? There have been so many, depending on where I happened to be standing in my life—a troubled teenager at prep school (Salinger's *Nine Stories*); an earnest undergrad in Chicago (Nabokov's *Pale Fire*); a high school teacher in Vermont (Calvino's *If on a winter's night a traveler*); a starving artist/graduate student in New York City (Faulkner's *As I Lay Dying*); an aspiring novelist (Cather's *The Professor's House*, Maxwell's *They Came Like Swallows*, Connell's *Mr. Bridge* and *Mrs. Bridge*)—all of them imperative, urgent, and somehow essential to my own circumstances at the time. With each book I was no longer alone, or rather, no longer felt lonely; through each book I escaped my own situation to live very, very far away.

As I recall, the book that first revealed this strange dichotomy to me—understanding what is real through what is entirely imagined—was *Charlotte's Web.*

"Where's Papa going with that ax?"

If students of writing need a structure to study, they'd be smart to look to the opening line of *Charlotte's Web.* How can you turn away? E. B. White grabs your hand and never lets go, from the shock of the question through the ensuing crisis and Fern's blossoming kinship with Wilbur and Charlotte and all the characters of the barnyard. The result is a page-turner of animal high jinks orchestrated by an ingenious spider, as well as a quixotic meditation on friendship and the passage of time. Just consider the brilliance of the ending: "Wilbur never forgot Charlotte. . . . It is not often that someone comes along who is a true friend and a good writer. Charlotte was both."

Years ago I studied with a teacher who announced one day, "Every great book is ultimately a metaphor for the very act of writing." At the time, I had no idea what he meant. Now I think I do.

I read *Charlotte's Web* when I was eight or nine years old. I lived in a suburb outside Orange, Texas, and knew nothing of farms, or fathers wielding axes. It mattered not a bit. I understood fairly quickly that I would never forget this story, that while it took place in the mud and musty barn of its own landscape, it somehow confirmed all my suspicions about the things of the world, and, in so doing, oddly though quite certainly confirmed me. I too wanted to shape words into stories that would be more than books; stories that would both reflect the reader's life and transport her to the universe of the imagination. Of course, I had no idea that's what I wanted to do—I just knew that *Charlotte's Web* was unlike anything I had ever read before, a book that was both a true friend and good writing.

Some pig.

KATE WALBERT is the author of *Our Kind*, a finalist for the 2004 National Book Award, *The Gardens of Kyoto*, and *Where She Went*. She lives in New York City with her family.

Edwin Mullhouse

STEVEN MILLHAUSER

KATHARINE WEBER

I read *Edwin Mullhouse* about a year after it came out. It was 1973, and I was seventeen, a freshman in an experimental college at the New School for Social Research. I bought a discounted hardcover copy at Penn Station in New York and read it on a train to New Haven, where I had been urgently summoned by my Yalie friend Rose, who suddenly required my contraceptive expertise. I was shocked when the train reached New Haven only moments into the journey, engrossed as I was in this novel that was so unlike any other novel I had ever read. *Edwin Mullhouse* was a biography of a child by another child!

But not really—this was something you could do, you could write a novel that said it was a biography of a child by another child. It was funny and important and moving, and it felt like something that had grown inside of me. The acknowledgments were deeply witty in a new way. Even the novel's jacket, a crayoned report cover, was unlike any other book jacket I had ever seen, and it was what prompted me to buy the book when I had only meant to buy gum.

New Haven was snowy and noticeably colder than New York, and we traipsed across campus to the Rexall Drug on the corner of High Street so I could supervise Rose's purchases. We ate dinner in Freshman Commons that night, and above the clatter and din I told her about the amazing book I was reading, and I heard myself say that this novel made me feel that I could write a novel myself. Rose understood. She herself was planning to publish many novels and was famous in high school for having written a few already.

We were very intellectual girls, Rose and I, though soon enough I would come to realize that most of what we had in common was a mutual fascination with her problems, which wasn't enough to sustain our friendship. That night, though, I was honored to be included in her drama of the moment, I was excited about *Edwin Mullhouse*, which I would finish on the train ride back to New York the next morning, and I wasn't yet guilty about the Heidegger text in my backpack, which made the round trip to New Haven unread, though the glare of disapproval beamed at me down the seminar table by my philosophy professor, Hannah Arendt herself, would be chastening the following day, and would haunt me from then to now.

I didn't do the reading for Hannah Arendt's class because I read Steven Millhauser's *Edwin Mullhouse* instead. She was disappointed and irritated by my poor judgment and apparent lack of commitment to scholarship, but *Edwin Mullhouse* gave me permission to write novels. I have written and published four so far. That's what I do. I write novels and I teach fiction writing.

I taught for eight years at Yale. The Rexall Drug is now an Au Bon Pain sandwich shop. I believe Rose is a real estate lawyer in New Jersey. As much as I really do regret my failure to prepare for that class, I cannot imagine that having Hannah Arendt not glare at me that afternoon would have been worth reading Heidegger on the train instead.

KATHARINE WEBER is the author of the novels *Triangle*, *The Little Women*, *The Music Lesson*, and *Objects in the Mirror Are Closer Than They Appear.* More information can be found at www.katharineweber.com.

The Great Gatsby

F. Scott Fitzgerald

Jacqueline Winspear

I can't say that a single book has ever changed my life as such, unless of course you count my first novel, *Maisie Dobbs.* Now, that changed everything, setting me on the path to a lifelong dream, that of being a full-time writer.

Many books have influenced my thinking, however, perhaps by bringing to life another culture, another time, extraordinary characters, or simply by providing an insight into the life lived every day by ordinary folk. I can point to one book that opened up a new world of literature for me: *The Great Gatsby*, by F. Scott Fitzgerald. Prior to checking it out of the library when I was seventeen or eighteen, I had been raised on a staple diet of the classics, followed by the likes of Evelyn Waugh, Somerset Maugham, E. M. Forster, Aldous Huxley, and George Orwell—all very typical of a British education. Then I read *The Great Gatsby*, which led me to a cadre of American authors. I virtually inhaled every book I could lay my hands on by Scott Fitzgerald, then Ernest Hemingway, John Dos Passos, John Steinbeck, William Faulkner, moving on to those who came later, such as Flannery O'Connor, Eudora Welty—the list was, thankfully, never ending. I read their novels, essays, letters. After reading Scott Fitzgerald's *Tender Is the Night*, I began wearing vintage clothing from the 1920s and 1930s. I listened to the music, immersing myself in the time, and was especially curious about the dark side of life between the wars. The title of my English dissertation, if I remember correctly, was "The Theory of Love As Portrayed by Scott Fitzgerald in *Tender Is the Night*, and Ernest Hemingway in *A Farewell to Arms.*" I was twenty years old, and I think I went on a bit about emotional bankruptcy. Oh dear, I'm blushing at the memory.

I was intrigued by those American authors because the writing was so *different*, from measured descriptive narrative to spare language. And I adored the reflection of the times, whether it was the exodus from the Midwest when America's bread basket turned into a dust bowl in *The Grapes of Wrath*, or the raw characters drawn in *U.S.A.* by Dos Passos.

The Great Gatsby gave me a quote that I first stuck on the wall of my room in the college residence, and is now scribbled on a Post-it above my computer: "So we beat on, boats against the current, borne back ceaselessly into the past."

JACQUELINE WINSPEAR's first novel, *Maisie Dobbs,* was a New York Times Notable Book of 2003, a Book Sense Top Ten Pick, and a *Publishers Weekly* Top Ten Mystery. *Maisie Dobbs* received seven award nominations and won the Agatha Award for Best First Novel, the Macavity Award for Best First Mystery Novel, and the Alex Award. The sequel, *Birds of a Feather*, was nominated for four awards and won the Agatha for Best Novel. Winspear's third novel, *Pardonable Lies*, has been nominated for two awards, and her fourth, *Messenger of Truth*, has just been published by Henry Holt.

The Books That Changed Their Lives

A Reading List of the Books Selected by the Contributors

Louisa May Alcott, *Little Women* / ANNE LAMOTT

Maya Angelou, *I Know Why the Caged Bird Sings* / SARK

Geoffrey Barraclough, *An Introduction to Contemporary History* / PAUL KENNEDY

John Barth, *The End of the Road* / JANE STERN

Ernest Becker, *The Denial of Death* / BENJAMIN CHEEVER, ROBERT KURSON

Peter Benchley, *Jaws* / CHRIS BOHJALIAN

The Bible / SENATOR JOE LIEBERMAN

William Peter Blatty, *The Exorcist* / CHRIS BOHJALIAN

Charlotte Brontë, *Jane Eyre* / MARGOT LIVESEY

Gwendolyn Brooks, *Selected Poems* / JAMES ATLAS

Dee Brown, *Bury My Heart at Wounded Knee* / SEBASTIAN JUNGER

Anthony Burgess, *A Clockwork Orange* / IAN RANKIN

Julius Caesar, *Caesar's Gallic Wars* / CAROLINE B. COONEY

Joseph Campbell, with Bill Moyers, *The Power of Myth* / ROBERT BALLARD

Albert Camus, *The Myth of Sisyphus* / JACQUES PÉPIN

Lewis Carroll, *Alice in Wonderland* / JACK PRELUTSKY

Lewis Carroll, *Through the Looking Glass* / JACK PRELUTSKY

G. K. Chesterton, *The Man Who Was Thursday* / ANNE PERRY

Mary Higgins Clark, *A Stranger Is Watching* / CAROL HIGGINS CLARK

Robert Coover, *Pricksongs & Descants* / KATE ATKINSON

John Crowley, *Little, Big* / HAROLD BLOOM

Ram Dass, *The Only Dance There Is* / ANNE LAMOTT

Charles Dickens, *David Copperfield* / MAUREEN CORRIGAN

Arthur Conan Doyle, *The Adventures of Sherlock Holmes* / LINDA FAIRSTEIN

Alexandre Dumas, *The Count of Monte Cristo* / DA CHEN

Guy Endore, *Voltaire! Voltaire!* / LIZ SMITH

F. Scott Fitzgerald, *The Great Gatsby* / FAITH MIDDLETON, JACQUELINE WINSPEAR

C. S. Forester, The Horatio Hornblower Series / PACO UNDERHILL

Sigmund Freud, *The Interpretation of Dreams* / BARBARA LEAMING

Moss Hart, *Act One* / FRANK RICH

Ernest Hemingway, *Collected Stories* / TRACY KIDDER

Ernest Hemingway, *For Whom the Bell Tolls* / SENATOR JOHN MCCAIN

John Hersey, *Hiroshima* / LARY BLOOM

Langston Hughes, *The Collected Poems* / ANNE LAMOTT

Aldous Huxley, *Brave New World* / NELSON DEMILLE

Susan Isaacs, *Compromising Positions* / SARA NELSON

Sebastian Junger, *The Perfect Storm* / LINDA GREENLAW

Carolyn Keene, The Nancy Drew Mysteries / CLAIRE COOK

Jean Kerr, *The Snake Has All the Lines* / GINA BARRECA

Søren Kierkegaard, *Fear and Trembling* / ANNE LAMOTT

Harper Lee, *To Kill a Mockingbird* / CHRIS BOHAJALIAN, WALLY LAMB, SUSAN VREELAND

Astrid Lindgren, *Pippi Longstocking* / ANNE LAMOTT

The Little Engine That Could / JEFF BENEDICT

Hugh Lofting, The Doctor Dolittle Series / RICHARD RHODES

William Maxwell, *So Long, See You Tomorrow* / STEWART O'NAN

Ed McBain, The 87th Precinct Series / LEIGH MONTVILLE

Frank McCourt, *Angela's Ashes* / LISA SCOTTOLINE

Thomas Merton, *The Seven Storey Mountain* / BROTHER CHRISTOPHER

Steven Millhauser, *Edwin Mullhouse* / KATHARINE WEBER

Christopher Morley, *Kitty Foyle* / LIZ SMITH

Toni Morrison, *The Bluest Eye* / DOROTHY ALLISON

Vladimir Nabokov, *Lolita* / BILLY COLLINS

William Lewis Nida, *Ab the Cave Man* / SHERWIN B. NULAND

Joyce Carol Oates, *Expensive People* / CHRIS BOHJALIAN

George Orwell, *Animal Farm* / NELSON DEMILLE

George Orwell, *1984* / NELSON DEMILLE

Ayn Rand, *Atlas Shrugged* / NELSON DEMILLE

Marjorie Kinnan Rawlings, *The Yearling* / BILLY COLLINS

Rainer Maria Rilke, *Letters to a Young Poet* / ALEXANDRA STODDARD

J. D. Salinger, *The Catcher in the Rye* / ELIZABETH BERG, ALICE HOFFMAN

William Saroyan, *The Human Comedy* / BERNIE S. SIEGEL

Albert Schweitzer, *Out of My Life and Thought* / RICHARD RHODES

The Sears Catalogue / MICHAEL STERN

Ernest Thompson Seton, *Wild Animals I Have Known* / JACK PRELUTSKY

William Shakespeare, *The Complete Works* / NICHOLAS A. BASBANES

William Shakespeare, *Henry VIII* / FRANK MCCOURT

Betty Smith, *A Tree Grows in Brooklyn* / JACQUELYN MITCHARD

Gertrude Stein, *Ida* / HARRIET SCOTT CHESSMAN

Stendhal, *The Red and the Black* / EDWARD SOREL

Robert Louis Stevenson, *A Child's Garden of Verses* / JACK PRELUTSKY

Harriet Beecher Stowe, *Uncle Tom's Cabin* / PATRICIA CORNWELL

Thomas à Kempis, *The Imitation of Christ* / CARLOS EIRE

Kay Thompson, *Eloise* / LAURA NUMEROFF

J. R. R. Tolkien, *The Lord of the Rings* / GRAEME BASE

Anthony Trollope, *The Way We Live Now* / DOMINICK DUNNE

Thomas Tryon, *Harvest Home* / CHRIS BOHJALIAN

Barbara W. Tuchman, *The Guns of August* / DORIS KEARNS GOODWIN

Sigrid Undset, *Kristin Lavransdatter* / TOMIE DEPAOLA

E. B. White, *Charlotte's Web* / KATE WALBERT

Theodore H. White, *The Making of the President, 1960* / STEVEN BRILL

P. G. Wodehouse, *The Most of P. G. Wodehouse* / AMY BLOOM

Cecil Woodham-Smith, *The Reason Why* / DAVID HALBERSTAM

Virginia Woolf, *A Room of One's Own* / ANITA DIAMANT

Herman Wouk, *Marjorie Morningstar* / SARA NELSON

Editors' Note

Billy Collins has it right—every book in some way changes your life. So after we asked all our incredibly generous contributors to single out one book in their essays, we've taken the undisciplined liberty of recommending dozens of books. We wish we could recommend hundreds. We've omitted the obvious choices—the books to be found on high school and college reading lists or on this or that Great Books list, like *The Odyssey* or *Anna Karenina*—as well as the books already discussed by our contributors or written by our contributors. (Of course you must read everything they've written!) Instead, we've focused on books you may have forgotten or may never have heard of. In the many cases where both of us chose the same book, only one of us has listed it, to avoid duplication. We freely admit that our lists are selective, subjective, quirky, and incomplete—opinionated.

Roxanne's Very Opinionated Reading List

Putting this list together reminded me why I came to open R.J. Julia Booksellers—because there were so many books I wanted to recommend. If you were to ask me tomorrow, the list would probably be different. Italo Calvino, in *Why Read the Classics?*, says, "The classics are books which exercise a particular influence, both when they imprint themselves on our imagination as unforgettable, and when they hide in the layers of memory disguised as the individual's or the collective unconscious." These words have guided my choices.

Fiction

Julia Alvarez, *In the Time of the Butterflies*

Saul Bellow, *Herzog*

Rosellen Brown, *Before and After*

Anthony Burgess, *Earthly Powers*

Albert Camus, *The Stranger*

Wilkie Collins, *The Woman in White*

Robertson Davies, *The Rebel Angels*

Ernest J. Gaines, *A Lesson Before Dying*

Nadine Gordimer, *July's People*

Julie Hecht, *Do the Windows Open?*

Ursula Hegi, *Stones from the River*

Milan Kundera, *The Unbearable Lightness of Being*

Jhumpa Lahiri, *Interpreter of Maladies*

Penelope Lively, *The Photograph*

Sándor Márai, *Embers*

Ian McEwan, *Atonement*

Lorrie Moore, *Who Will Run the Frog Hospital?*

V. S. Naipaul, *A Bend in the River*

Cynthia Ozick, *The Shawl*

José Saramago, *Blindness*

Mary Shelley, *Frankenstein*

William Styron, *Sophie's Choice*

Lawrence Thornton, *Imagining Argentina*

Leo Tolstoy, *Resurrection*

Richard Yates, *Revolutionary Road*

Émile Zola, *Thérèse Raquin*

Women's Lives

John Bayley, *Elegy for Iris*

Blanche Wiesen Cook, *Eleanor Roosevelt*

Kim Chernin, *In My Mother's House*

Elzbieta Ettinger, *Rosa Luxemburg*

Doris Grumbach, *Fifty Days of Solitude*

Margaret Mead, *Blackberry Winter*

Honor Moore, *The White Blackbird*

Phyllis Rose, *Parallel Lives*

Phyllis Rose, ed., *The Norton Book of Women's Lives*

Henri Troyat, *Catherine the Great*

Sojourner Truth, *The Narrative of Sojourner Truth*

Eudora Welty, *One Writer's Beginnings*

Lynne Withey, *Dearest Friend*

More Lives

Henry Adams, *The Education of Henry Adams*

Karen Armstrong, *Muhammad: A Biography of the Prophet*

Sarah Bradford, *Disraeli*

William Manchester, *The Last Lion: Winston Spencer Churchill*

Edmund Morris, *The Rise of Theodore Roosevelt*

Christopher Nolan, *Under the Eye of the Clock*

Tobias Wolff, *This Boy's Life*

Books About Issues

Martha Tod Dudman, *Augusta Gone*

Kay Redfield Jamison, *An Unquiet Mind: A Memoir of Moods and Madness*

Bernard Lefkowitz, *Our Guys: The Glen Ridge Rape and the Secret Life of the Perfect Suburb*

J. Anthony Lukas, *Common Ground: A Turbulent Decade in the Lives of Three American Families*

Adrian Nicole, *Random Family: Love, Drugs, Trouble, and Coming of Age in the Bronx*

Luis J. Rodriguez, *Always Running: La Vida Loca; Gang Days in L.A.*

Mark Salzman, *True Notebooks: A Writer's Year at Juvenile Hall*

Books I Read and Reread and Keep Always Near at Hand

Viktor E. Frankl, *Man's Search for Meaning*

Marcus Aurelius, *The Meditations of Marcus Aurelius*

Elizabeth Hauge Sword, ed., *A Child's Anthology of Poetry*

Rosamund Stone Zander and Benjamin Zander, *The Art of Possibility*

Joy's Very Opinionated Reading List

Being infinitely more disciplined than Roxanne, I've restricted myself to a small selection of my favorite fiction. Being an editor, I've added my two cents (and sometimes someone else's) about each book.

Harriet Arnow, *The Dollmaker.* The story of Gertie Nevels, backwoods woman from the Kentucky hills, fierce mother, determined wife, carver of wood. "Our most unpretentious American masterpiece," writes Joyce Carol Oates, "a brutal, beautiful novel."

Pat Barker, The Regeneration Trilogy (*Regeneration, The Eye in the Door, The Ghost Road*). A masterwork on the human costs of war, with the poet-soldiers Siegfried Sassoon and Wilfred Owen figuring among the vivid cast of real and fictional characters.

Andre Biely, *St. Petersburg.* The mordantly funny and brilliant tale of a high Tsarist official and his dilettante son, an aspiring terrorist whose first assignment is to assassinate a high Tsarist official. "One of the four great masterpieces of twentieth-century prose," in Nabokov's opinion.

Elizabeth Bowen, *The Little Girls.* Three schoolgirls bury a box, go their separate ways, and are brought together as adults by the box and its secrets—a mystery raised to a transcendent plane by

Bowen's inimitable style, shrewd psychological insight, and wicked humor.

Rebecca Brown, *The Gifts of the Body.* A spare, haunting novel narrated by a home-care worker who takes us on her rounds as she assists people with AIDS and becomes their companion in the everyday gestures that sustain life in the face of death.

Michael Cunningham, *Specimen Days.* The spirit of Walt Whitman presides over these three linked novellas: a ghost tale set in the 1800s, a present-day thriller, and a futuristic story that will make you fall in love with a green lizard woman from the planet Nadia.

John Derbyshire, *Seeing Calvin Coolidge in a Dream.* The story of Chai, a disillusioned Red Guard who flees China and settles in New York with his wife, the redoubtable Ding. "A masterpiece of style and a fine entertainment. . . . This astonishing first novel approaches perfection," says *The Boston Globe.*

Karen Joy Fowler, *The Sweetheart Season.* In case the rousing success of *The Jane Austen Book Club* didn't inspire you to read everything Fowler's written, don't miss this one, her second novel, chronicling the triumphs and defeats of the Sweetwheat Sweethearts all-girl baseball team.

Rhoda Huffey, *The Hallelujah Side.* A wonderfully funny novel about a little girl growing up in a Pentecostal family, with one of the all-time best first sentences: "It had been a Second Coming sky all day, which meant they might be in heaven by this evening."

Zora Neale Hurston, *Mules and Men.* A landmark collection of black America's folklore—tall tales, fairy tales, and jokes, sermons, songs, superstitions, "them big old lies we tell when we're jus' sittin' around here on the store porch doin' nothin'."

Kazuo Ishiguro, *The Remains of the Day.* A tour de force about the class system, duty, honor, and the warring impulses of the human heart.

Harley Jane Kozak, *Dating Dead Men.* Sheer pleasure, witty, smart, sexy, suspenseful, winner of the Agatha, Anthony, and Macavity awards for best first mystery novel.

Ursula K. Le Guin, *Searoad.* These chronicles of Klatsand, a little town on the Oregon coast, show another side of Le Guin, best known for her science fiction, but a master storyteller in any genre. "In and Out" and "Bill Weisler" are among the finest stories I know.

Rosina Lippi, *Homestead.* The intertwined lives of the villagers of Rosenau, a remote speck of a town in the Austrian Alps, make for a novel of tremendous power and depth, winner of the 1998 PEN-Hemingway Award for best first fiction.

Colum McCann, *Everything in This Country Must.* A novella and two stories about the Troubles in Northern Ireland, told in prose that "flows with a lean, austere majesty" and yields "a shivery, hard-earned, unforgettable beauty" (Dan Cryer, *Newsday*).

Tim O'Brien, *The Things They Carried.* A harrowing, beautifully rendered journey into the mud and moral confusions of the Vietnam War, with the recitation of what the men carried serving as an eloquent mantra of hope and loss, longing and love.

Tillie Olsen, *Tell Me a Riddle.* Four luminous, heartbreaking stories of unsurpassed power. "When she wrote *Tell Me a Riddle,* Tillie Olsen, like William Blake, covered paper with words 'for the angels to read,'" says John Leonard.

Grace Paley, *The Collected Stories.* Oh, what tales from our Homer of ordinary life, what deeds and misdeeds, what personalities. Oh, what a voice, from beginning—"I was popular in certain circles, says Aunt Rose. I wasn't no thinner then, only more stationary in the flesh"—to end.

Paul Scott, The Raj Quartet (*The Jewel in the Crown, The Day of the Scorpion, The Towers of Silence, A Division of Spoils*). Scott's epic of the British rule of India, filled with superbly realized characters and brimming with event, is both unforgettable fiction and one of the most powerful indictments of racism and colonialism ever put to paper.

Héctor Tobar, *The Tattooed Soldier.* The fates of two displaced men—one a member of a Guatemalan death squad, the other a man whose family he murdered—converge against the backdrop of the L.A. riots in a novel as revealing as it is riveting.

About Read to Grow

Read to Grow is a Connecticut nonprofit organization that distributes literacy packets and new books to families of newborns in seven urban hospitals, and redistributes books from communities with a surplus to communities with a need. We are 100 percent donor-supported, and rely on a large volunteer corps to assist a part-time staff in operating our programs.

Read to Grow is unique. We associate early literacy with health by beginning our work with families in the hospital when babies are born and parents' aspirations are high. Our message to new parents is that they are their baby's first and most important teacher, that they hold the key to linking love and learning, and that they already have the tools they need. We provide information about how books and the sharing of early language are critical to their child's cognitive and emotional development. We tell them that when they hold, talk to, and share books with their children, they are reinforcing a positive approach to reading and language, and fostering an embrace of lifelong learning.

We currently work in four regions of the state and operate a variety of hospital- and community-based programs. With the assistance of trained volunteers and hospital nursing staff, the Books for Babies Program distributes the literacy packets for parents and the new books for their infants. The Books for Babies Follow-up Program provides additional books and literacy information twice during a baby's first year of life. Books for

Kids encourages family literacy by making books more accessible to parents with limited resources and to the health and educational organizations that serve them. The Pediatric Waiting Room Reading Program models read-aloud techniques for caregivers while engaging children in the joy of reading. The toll-free Connecticut Library Hotline provides information on the state's two hundred libraries as well as reading tips and resources for families.

We know we are making a difference in the lives of Connecticut children and their families. In the past year, several hospitals across the state have contacted us to bring our programming into their maternity units. The number of families who have received our materials and contacted us to request books and guidance in choosing appropriate ones has doubled. We field phone calls from clinics, schools, child-care centers, and individuals asking for books. We receive letters thanking us for our message, our programs, and the gift of books. One mother wrote, "I have never read to a baby before until I read to my daughter. At first it was embarrassing but now I'm used to it. She loves it and I love reading to her. Keep up the good work. God bless." Another letter began, "Dear Book Friend," and described a classroom of children hugging what were, for many, the first books they'd ever owned. And another: "Thank you for helping my son learn about colors and pictures and the world through books." At Read to Grow we help families teach their children to learn. By connecting books, words, and shared time, parents connect language and learning with love.

To find out more about Read to Grow, log on to www.readtogrow.org. And thanks for supporting our work through your purchase of this book.

LAURIE E. RUDERFER,
EXECUTIVE DIRECTOR

Acknowledgments

I am tempted to thank everyone who ever spoke a kind or encouraging word to me, starting with my mom and going right on up to the sweet garage attendant who wished me a good day this morning, but in the interest of brevity I will thank only those who made this book possible.

The Book That Changed My Life was conceived as a celebration of the fifteenth birthday of R.J. Julia Booksellers, my bookstore in Madison, Connecticut, and of the thousands of readers who have attended events at the store to meet authors and talk about books. All of the contributors are people who have appeared at R.J. Julia over the years, and I thank them first and foremost for their wonderful essays, which they graciously agreed to donate so that the profits from this book could in turn be donated to Read to Grow.

I originally envisioned a kind of fancy pamphlet that we would put together at the store and give to our customers, an idea that might have langished on my to-do list if I hadn't mentioned it to Bill Shinker, president and publisher of Gotham Books. He loved the idea and envisioned it as the elegant book you're now holding. Bill's staff at Gotham shares his passion for and clarity about publishing, and I am deeply grateful to them, particularly to senior editor Erin Moore for guiding the whole project with her calm, lovely intelligence; to art director Ray Lundgren for his beautiful design and his endless patience; to marketing director Lisa Johnson for her expertise and enthusiasm; to publicist Beth Parker for her energy and creativity; to managing editor Susan Schwartz and her department for their care with the manuscript; and to assistant editor Jessica Sindler for all her invaluable help.

Running a bookstore today is a labor of love, and R.J. Julia has been blessed with a staff whose passion for their work extends to tracking a book down when all the customer knows is that it has a blue cover and the title begins with *The*. I thank them all, and especially Anne Pember, who makes it all happen; Karen Corvello, who brilliantly manages the store, making sure it's got the books, the looks, and the energy that our customers love; Debbie Brooke, who wisely and with great humor takes incredible care of our staff and customers; Nancy Brown, who knows every answer to any question about any book; Maggie Cohn, whose thoughtfulness always helps us make better decisions; Kathryn Fabiani, who takes on any project anyone asks for, and does it with enthusiasm and intelligence; Joanna Zygmont and Marybeth Sydor, who were tirelessly resourceful in coordinating the details of this project; and of course Linda Hill, our events queen, who has brought so many amazing writers to the store.

I also want to thank Esther Newberg and Kari Stuart, my agents, for their able representation; the many publicists, editors, and agents who helped us enlist our contributors; Gina Barreca, Alix Boyle, Faith Middleton, and Karen Pritzker, who offered not only their friendship and support but a fine editorial eye and advice that helped me refine and crystallize thoughts that started out messy; Lisa Maass and Caroline Wharton, whom I speak with almost every morning, and who always have wisdom when I need it and wicked wit when they're tired of my being serious—they can always make me laugh; Marilyn Nyman, my friend of more than forty years, who is always grounding, understanding, and smart; Mark Salter, who gave me a haven and his sage advice when I was at the last of my deadlines and could delay no more; the Read to Grow staff and board, who with their passion and commitment are making a meaningful difference in the lives of children and their families; R.J. Julia's customers, who have supported us and contributed to making our community a place where words matter; and the town of Madison, Scranton Library, Polson Middle School, and Academy School for always opening their doors to welcome our authors and audiences.

Above all else, I thank my husband, Kevin, and my son, Edward, otherwise known as my boys, whom I love to the sky and beyond.

R. J. C.

I join Roxanne in thanking the contributors for their generosity, and for the privilege of having been their editor for the space of a few hundred words. I join her too in thanking Bill, Erin, and everyone at Gotham for the unalloyed pleasure of working with them. And to Jo and Sydelle, Dawn, Maria and Stan, Alicia and Rathin, Dorothy, Leslie, Harley, Ellie, Ursula, Gladys, Karen, Alice, Nancy and Edna, Faith and Fern, Elizabeth and Nick, Carlos and Lilly, Carol, the Halls, Sarah, Caitlin, and Alex, thanks beyond measure and beyond words.

J. J.